Fir-Bob Land

A Look Round

Higher Bebington

by

Allan Alsbury

To Vera,

[signature]

First Published 1999 by Countyvise Limited, 14 Appin Road,
Birkenhead, CH41 9HH.

Briitsh Library Cataloguing in Publication Data.
A catalogue record for this book is available from the British Library.

ISBN 1 901231 17 8

ii

The Author.

Allan Alsbury came to Wirral from his home town of Derby in 1951 to work in Unilever Research at Port Sunlight. When he married Dorothy in 1954 they moved to one of the newly built houses in Mill Road.With his interest in Local History and as a keen amateur photographer he has, over the years, looked into several areas and aspects of yesteryear. From the information gathered he has given talks to local Societies and Groups in the Merseyside and North Wales areas. He has previously published "Christ's Church, Higher Bebington:1895-1989".

Contents

Acknowledgments.

My thanks are due to all those who have talked with me about the village and its life, it is not possible to mention them all individually.
The Staff of Wirral Libraries, and Cheshire Records Office, in Chester, have given valuable help, often offering suggestions for further lines of enquiry much further afield.

Corrections & Addenda.

Contents:

     'Acknowledgements', should be 'page vii'.
     'Preface',   should be 'page xi'.
Insert, 'Introduction............................ pagexvii'.
     Under '9', page vi, add sub-heading,
       'Christ's Church.............. page 118'

Page   xx, Beginning of second para should read,
         'The plan on page xv...'
Page   xx, from last sentence delete, '...on page xii..'
Page   8, Next to last para should end, '...Police Force.
     In 1939, when he was Deputy Cheif Constable,
     he was awarded the MBE. He lived to be 92.'
     Delete 'He lived to be ninety two' that follows.
Page   13, Line 1, '...Village Road is quite narrow...'
Page   94, Caption should read, '...John Whieldon...'
Page   103, 1st line, 2nd para should read, '...junction
     of Bracken Lane and Red Hill Road...'
Page   120, Caption should read, '...before the Rood
     was installed.

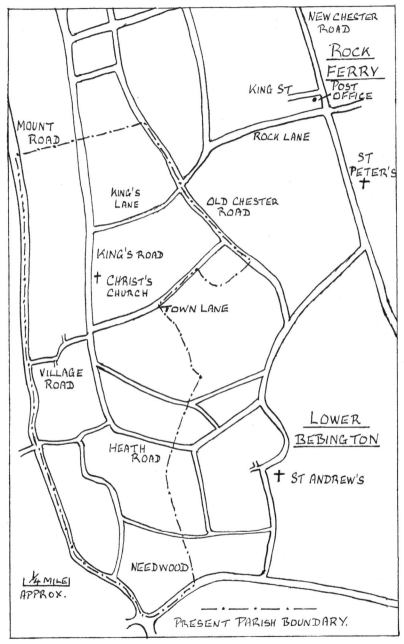

Administrative area of Higher Bebington in the 19th Century

Preface

I came to Higher Bebington in 1954, to live in Mill Road. Very soon, I began to look around the village to see just what was there.There was the tower of an old windmill, several older cottages, old inns and an extensive area of quarrying. When I looked in likely books for some information about the village, I was rather disappointed. Larger works regarded the village as being mainly based on the area we now regard as the separate Rock Ferry, in fact White's Directory for 1860 says,- "Bebington (Higher or Superior) is a small village and township which also comprises the populous district of Rock Ferry", and goes on to say that "The Post Office is at Mr Dakin's in King Street",(that is, in Rock Ferry).

The Higher Bebington Local Board was established in 1859 and its office was also in King Street and at the time I was looking into this their carved stone emblem was still in place in the wall of a house that by then was a plumber's depot.

The Rock Ferry area of the township was part of the original manorial lands which gave access to the river for fishing rights and transport by sea. The establishment here in the early part of the 19th C of a residential area for Liverpool merchants put it in a totally different light.

In 1842 a splendid Church, St.,Peter on the Rock, in Rock Ferry had been built to serve the whole combined area.The only real concession to the true village lay in brief mention of there being quarries that provided good quality building stone.

From the way Rock Park developed, even by as early as 1860 with 45 houses, 26 of them being the homes of Liverpool merchants, the connections between this area and the orginal village were becoming tenuous. They were two distinct communities. Even the establishment of St Peter's Church at Rock Ferry did little to unite them, it was nearly a two mile walk from the village, twice as far as to St Andrew's in Lower Bebington. It was far more logical that Rock Ferry should become part of Birkenhead, and in 1877 it was ceded to them by the then Urban District Council of Higher Bebington. The village thus returned, at least for a time, to its original semi-rural way of life and individuallity.

Digressing slightly, I remember as a child listening to a programme on 'The Wireless' presented by 'NOMAD' the pen name of the naturalist and author Norman Ellison. What should I find but that he lived in Caldy and, had recently written a book on 'WIRRAL', so I consulted it. He did include Higher Bebington as the separate village that I sought, but some of his observations left my pride in my newly acquired habitat rather dented. He mentioned visiting an old Inn, 'The Royal Oak', and the quarries that in the last century had yielded wonderful fossil impressions of prehistoric animals footsteps but, of the village itself he did not appear very impressed from the comments he made and I quote them:

The village is such a hotch potch of mean and featurelesss cottages, many built of the local stone, that it needs but passing mention here. .the derelict stump of the windmill fits admirably into the general picture.

In view of this I discussed it with him. He made the point that he was a naturalist rather than an historian and had tended to slant his work on this basis. Also, he had tended to look, not only at Higher Bebington but other villages, from the generally rather romantic view of 'The Typical English Village', centred round a village green, with an old Inn, hence his visit to The Royal Oak, and a Church that reflects the history of the village over the centuries. In conclusion, he asked me not to use the quotation from his work without an explanation such as this, as he himself felt it would be unfair to such an old established, hard working community.

Unfortunately, some authors have quoted him out of context, particularly after his death when he could not be consulted, so perhaps I can help to put his thoughts in the right context. The image of Higher Bebington has also suffered on many occasions from the quoting out of context of remarks made by Nathanial Hawthorne, the author and American Consul in Liverpool in 1853, from his "English Notebooks". He describes a walk with his family during which they see, "——one cottage which I suppose was several hundred years old; it was of stone, filled into a wooden framework, the black oak of which was visible like a skeleton; it had a thatched roof and was whitewashed. We passed through a village (Higher Bebington, I believe) with narrow streets, and mean houses, all of brick or stone, not standing wide apart from each other, as in American country villages, but all conjoined." If the remainder of the paragraph is read it is quite certain that he was describing Lower Bebington village at the junction of The Grove and The Village at the bottom of Heath Road.

I started talking with some of the people whose families I believed had lived in the village for a considerable time, and soon started to get some interesting views of life in the village. As well as this I also managed to collect a few pictures of the the village in the past, and take photographs as it is today. Combining these I was able to put together an illustrated talk, the result of which was that people came to me afterwards giving me even more information and told of their work and their lives.

Some people have suggested that I should put my findings into print, well, that is what I have tried to do. But it is not my story, it is that of Higher Bebington and Fir-Bobs, all I have done is to collect it together.

Finally, do remember the frailty of the human memory; it is not unusual for two people knowing the same 'facts' from personal experience to see and remember them in very different lights. Then there is the problem of putting together other peoples' recollections into the right perspective. Many times after I have given a talk someone has said to me, "But you didn't say anything about so-and-so.", or "You are wrong about————, it was like this,————." I am sure you will make similar comments on my errors and omissions; please forgive them, your help in improving the situation will always be appreciated.

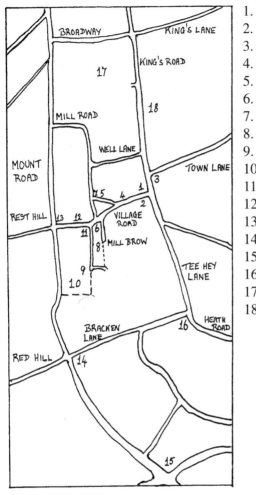

Higher Bebington Village

1. King's Farm
2. Old Hall Farm
3. King's Yard
4. Royal Oak
5. Smithy
6. 'George Hotel'
7. Holly Hall Cottage
8. The Windmill
9. The Old Schools
10. The Quarries
11. 'The Tiny Inn'
12. The Steam Mill
13. 'The Travellers' Rest'
14. Brackenwood House
15. Needwood Farm
16. Gorsey Hey
17. Higher Bebington Hall
18. Christ's Church

Introduction

You have probably seen many books that carry titles such as.
'The Complete Book of...........'
'The Encyclopedia of..............'
'Everything You Should Know About.......'
and have been rather disappointed when the answers to many of your
questions are not there. Well, you have seen the title I have used is simply "A Look Around Higher Bebington" and that is all it is . It covers
some of the history,some of the geography,some of the life, but it does
not pretend to be exhaustive - that would be far too much and I don't
think it would make enjoyable reading.

One important point that must be made before we go any further, the
name *Fir-Bob* and" *Fir-Bob Land*" when refering to Higher
Bebington. Fir-bob Land comes from the profusion of fir-cones that are
found in the woods on the ridge above the village, and hence a Fir-bob
is the term used to describe an inhabitant of the village. But, not just
any inhabitant. To be a Fir-Bob one needs to be a descendent of a family whose roots go back in the history of the village.

An incomer like myself would not presume to describe themselves
as a Fir-bob. This was brought home to me on one occasion in 1964
when I asked Mr.John Nixon, who I knew had been a Churchwarden
for many years and his wife who, in her earlier years had been in service in one of the 'Big Houses', if I might talk to him sometime about
life in the village. He replied, "Oh no, its no good asking me, you see
I'm a Frodsham man, I've only lived here since 1895".

What's in a name, as they say? There are many works devoted to
Place Names and often considerable discussion as to name derivations.
Looking at *Bebington* or *Bebbington* as it has been spelt, the usual
finding is that " The name is almost certainly Anglo-Saxon in origin;
Bebba was probably a Saxon Chief, and his kinsmen and followers
made up the tribe of the Bebbing. Thus, the town's name originally sig-
nified the '*Ton*' or homestead of the Bebbing."That is about as far as
one gets. But who was Bebba, you ask? Was he anyone of importance,
or merely a minor land-owner?

Let's go back to the latter part of the 6th century, and look a little wider. The kingdom of Northumbria was ruled by Ethelfrith of Bernicia from 593-616 AD, and like his antecedents he had ambitions to bring wider areas to the South under his Lordship. The Bernicians had already spread their influence, it is believed more by diplomacy than by conquest, across the country to the Solway Firth by the year 580 AD, and soon established themselves on the Cumbrian coast.

From the evidence of place names in Cumberland and Lancashire there is ample evidence that they continued to move right down to the Mersey. About 613 AD, Ethelfrith made an expedition into North-west Cheshire, and sought out the Britons at Caerlegion (Chester). The Britons were led by Solomon, son of Cynan, King of Pòwys, and were attended by over 1000 monks from Bangor-Isa-Coed to pray for the Briton's victory, but in the event Ethelfrith's men slew all but 50 of the monks, and the Britons were heavily defeated in the battle that followed.

Having brought his forces this far and achieved victory, it seems reasonable to suppose that the Bernicians would have established settlements of their own and also taken over existing villages and renamed them . Now, Ethelfrith's wife was BEBBA, and it was quite common, if not normal practice, for places to be named in relation to a woman, particularly the wife of a Leader or King. It seems a reasonable assumption then that Bebbington owes its name to Queen Bebba the Bernician. This would seem a more realistic derivation than an unqualified attribution to "a Saxon chief called Bebba". That Bebba's name was used in naming of a settlement is evidenced by the following points

Ethelfrith's home was at Din Guayrdi, to give it its original Celtic name. This fortress (DIN=Fort) was where his Grandfather,King Ida, had established the Bernician Royal household in 547 AD, and it was known as "The Royal City".Later, as described by The Venerable Bede in his 'Ecclesiastical History', the name was changed to BEBBAN-BURGH or Bebba's Fortress after Ethelfrith's wife. From this we get, by simple corruption, the modern name of that most imposing fortress, BAMBURGH and the adjacent village. It looks, then, that we in Bebington, have a 'Twin' village in Northumberland!

It is from this naming after BEBBA that the original spelling with the double 'B' arises. Some people, particularly those not familiar with the area and the modern form with a single 'B' , still use the double 'B'. The double 'B' also persists in the spelling of the personal surname.

Today, Bebington is generally seen as the name of a very extensive administrative district. With the continuity of housing, the borders between the different parts, though marked by signs on the main roads, tend to be somewhat blurred in most people's minds. In the 19th cenury the Parish of Bebington was comprised of Lower Bebington, Higher Bebington, Poulton-cum-Spital, Storeton, and Tranmere townships each of a similar area, which were readily distinguished, each being modest sized communities with open land separating them. Their inhabitants, however, proudly guarding their individuallity.

The two Bebingtons have been distinguished in many ways over the years, Lower Bebington variously named as Great, Church, Kirk, Inferior, Subterior, Nether, The Lower Part of-, The Part With A Church, and Loer (Hearth Taxes, 1663), whilst Higher Bebington has been called Little, Superior, Over, Upper, Parva, The Smaller Part Of-, The Higher Part Of-, and Ou' Bebington (Hearth Taxes,1663).

It has often been asked,"Why two Bebingtons?". Probably the best answer to this would be to say, "Look at them not as two separate villages (which we have to concede they became) but as their names imply, " *Lower* and *Higher Bebingtons.*" Bebington, now Lower, was the original village; their needs included milling and under Manorial law they would have their own mill. The lands on which they grew their grains was almost entirely to the West and North of the village, so what better place for the mill than on the ridge to catch the winds to best advantage?

Stone had been taken from this ridge for some centuries, probably on a fairly casual basis as it was needed for specific works, before the Bebing-ton was established. But men skilled in doing this would need to be fairly permanently settled near to the ridge, and though extraction was almost entirely then on the Storeton side, the Eastern side of the ridge would provide a less exposed area in which to live, and reasonable line of communication with the 'Lower' village. This would have been along Kirk-Gate, or Church Gate, the Saxon trackway down which the stone was brought for the building of the Whit-(or White, from the colour of the stone) Church in Bebington, leading onto The Heath Road. Until recent years the remains of this track could be seen alongside the present Kirket Lane.

So, a settlement sprang up on the lee side of the ridge, and it would not be unreasonable for these people to be known as the Higher Bebington(ians)!

The community would have needed what today we call 'service Industries' too; farms to provide food, a smith and wheelwright for a start. These were on the Eastern edge of the village, what is now the junction of Village Road, Tee Hey Lane (as a continuation of 'The' Heath Road) and Town Lane.

The Plan on the opposite page shows the main area of the Village, and I suggest we take a walk round, starting from the present shopping centre at the junctions of Tee Hey Lane with Village Road and Town Lane. Some of the points of interest on the way are numbered in order on the Plan, so it will be easy to follow the route. From the centre of the village, we will go up Village Road looking along Mill Road and then to the mill, along School Lane, see where the quarries were. After reaching the top of Village Road we will go South along Mount Road, as far as Wishing Gate, then have a look at Brackenwood before going to the Southern end of the Parish by junction 4 of the M53. Back from there via Gorsey Hey, along Tee Hey Lane/King's Road to King's Close and finally to the Church.

You can trace this on the sketch map of the village on page xii, which shows the locations of some of the places we shall visit.

1

The Centre of the Village

Well, let's wander round Higher Bebington and see what there is, and what there has been. The best place to start is at the present 'centre' by the shops on Tee Hey Lane where it is joined by Village Road and Town Lane. Now much widened and straightened, up to 1931 it was only a rough track with a dog-leg at the Town Lane junction. If you had needed to take your farm cart further towards Birkenhead along King's Road (Mr King's road) you had to get the key from King's Farm, to the gate that was just beyond what is now Broadway. It was his road, as far as Cavendish Drive which was as far as the trams then came. Although Mr King after whom it, and other items were named, had long gone, the propriety over this road and King's Lane was still guarded by the agents of the King estates, well into the 20th C. Prior to the King's coming to live in the village, this track was called Broad Lane, hence the naming of 'Broadway' later. Till then it was little more than a farm track, very muddy in wet weather, and quite a walk, on foot. It came past the brick-fields just inside the Parish boundary, where the boys of the village liked to go to fish for 'tiddlers' in the ponds there. King's Road was not fully made-up and 'Adopted' until 1932. We shall see more of the King family, who had large landownings in this area and in other parts of Wirral, as we go on.Today it is "The Acorn" that immediately catches the eye. The site on which it stands was, until 1934, King's Farm, which had lands along the King's Road towards Birkenhead.

King's Farm

As generally remembered, the main farm-house is described as having been built in 1734 by Inglefield. There was a date tablet over the

1

central front door with the initials *C and I, I, 1734,*which is taken to be for Charles Inglefield and his wife ,Isabella. It has been suggested that some parts of the design on this tablet were Masonic symbols, indicating that it was used as a meeting house. This dating refers to the main house as it is generally seen, say, on old photographs, but parts of it were much older, as its tenants have pointed out. Part of the house on its Northern side were probably built by William Inglefield about 1640-45 when he married. The Inglefields (Englefields) came from Stanford in the Vale (Whitmore Valley) and had connections with Thurstaston Hall. There was certainly a farm on this site in 1520 and from comparison with similar additions and extensions to cottages in the village it seems likely that the Northernmost end which was of cruck construction dated from 15th C or even earlier, and formed the original farm.

King's Farm in 1932: From a watercolour by Burnett

There must have been a farm there before 1734 because Oliver Cromwell is reputed to have spent three nights there in 1644 before his assault on Birkenhead Priory. However, he is said to have spent those nights in so many different cottages in Wirral that we can not put too much weight on that evidence. This main house, facing onto Tee Hey Lane almost opposite the top of Town Lane, was two-storied, pebble-dashed and regularly whitewashed. At the back of the site, abutting onto the boundary that now separates it from Victoria Hall were large stone built barns and stabling,with the main yard between them and the house, and a gateway opening onto Village Road. Many people referred to it as Pear Tree Farm; it never had this name, but it arose from the very large pear tree that grew on the Southern end wall of the house which presented a beautiful picture each spring when it was in blossom, to the extent that it was often the subject of local artists such as Burnett. And it yielded quite good crops of fruit. This tree must have been of considerable age; at the time the farm was demolished in the mid 1930's one resident who was then in his late 80's could just recollect it being planted when he was a young boy.

During the second half of 19th C the farm was tenanted by George Pate, who was an active member of the National Farmers' Union,and his family. In 1904 he moved to Storeton Hall Farm where he stayed until he died in 1926 .Mr Thomas Smailes took over King's farm when Mr Pate left; apart from the usual crops and animals, Mr Smailes worked a lot with poultry. There was always a good flock of ducks at the farm, twenty would be the minimum. There had been, up till just before Mr Pate left, a duck-pond at the farm. It was at the corner where the raised bed of flowers has now been placed on the pavement by the Council, but for some reason he filled it in. This meant that King's Farm ducks took a walk across Village Road early each morning and spent their day on the pond at Old Hall Farm, which was at the top end of their yard just below the terrace houses, returning 'home' at night. Relations were strained on one occasion when the gate at Old Hall farm was closed before the ducks returned and they had to spend the night there. That in itself was of no great consequence, but of course during the night about two dozen eggs were laid and these went into the Old Hall stock, rather than to King's Farm.

Towards the end of the year the poultry stock was greatly increased in readiness for the Christmas market. This stock came from Ireland, via the boats to Birkenhead. Transport as we know it did not exist and

3

Mr Smailes would walk down to Woodside, collect his stock of turkeys and geese, a flock of 100 or more, and walk them up Happy Valley and on the often muddy track that passed for a road, right up to the farm, where they were fattened up for the market.

The Smailes family were remembered by many in the village long after they had left in the 1930's. One of Mrs Smailes' sons, Edward, was ordained and taught at Birkenhead School. From his energetic ways he was often called 'The Battling Parson'. On many occasions he was invited to take services at Christ Church and was of considerable help during *interregna,* and was referred to with affection as Ted Smailes. Over the following 40 years Mrs Smailes would come with him when he took services and enjoy renewing acquaintances. Perhaps with these associations we can be forgiven if the farm has been referred to as 'Smailes' farm'.When I first met Mrs Smailes she and Ted lived in Caldy, in a house with quite a large garden. Although in her late 80's she still looked after the garden and baked their bread, which was delicious. They kept a loft of pigeons and once a week the evening meal would be a baked pigeon each. Mrs Smailes had a sharp memory; on one occasion I showed her a postcard view of the farm with four young children in the foreground and said that as the postmark was 1913 the photograph had probably been taken about 1910. " Oh, no" she said, at once, "It was taken in 1905, I can remember it was a Thursday afternoon." And she went on to identify each of the children as Dick, Tom, Harold and Hilda, older brothers and sister of Ted Smailes. A rather unusual expertise that Mrs Smailes retained throughout her life which was much in demand by the children when she lived in the village was that she could very quickly get just the right length and weight for the tail on any kite that the children might make to get it to fly properly. I am sure that many parents who have been frustrated in trying to do this would appreciate how her help was valued. After the Smailes left the Southerns were at the farm for a short time until it finally closed.

I remember as a child that my Mother, who came from Worcestershire, used to tell me of a saying they had there, which she assured me was based on an old custom; that was "To put the pig on the wall to watch the band go by". This, she told me, referred to regarding as of great importance some local event, like a procession or the visit of a minor local dignitary of no great consequence, that for

4

those involved was an important occasion. Well, I found that in Higher Bebington they really did 'Put the pig on the wall' in the literal sense. This happened for various events, most noticably on Whit Mondays when the local Lodge of the Friendly Society,(more of them later) had their annual 'Walk'. A suckling pig from King's farm would be dressed up with a fancy hat on and held on top of the farm wall with great jubilation as the band and procession went on its way. Many of those involved would be dressed in as comic outfits as was the pig! This ritual had certainly taken place since the latter part of the 19th century and continued as long as King's farm was working.

With the energetic expansion and developments in the area in the 1930's King's farm was sold to be demolished and the site redeveloped. It was proposed at one time that a Super Cinema should be built there. With the inevitable delays and the onset of WW2 this never materialised and the site remained as on open space until 1960 when 'The Acorn' was built. When this was being done, one Church leader was very outspoken about 'The gilded Gin Palace arising in our midst'. Now, apart from a single stone gatepost, only memories of the farming past remain.

Vine Farm.

Immediately to the North of King's farm was Vine Farm. This looked more or less directly down Town Lane. Matthew Horne was the farmer there and he too had poultry, they were his main work. At the farm he also had a coal business. The farm life came to an end in 1937 when it was pulled down, along with the other 'improvements' that were being made in the village.

Old Hall Farm.

The building of another farm that was working here still stands and is a 'Scheduled' building: it is now 'The Royal British Legion' Club. This is on the Southern corner of the junction of Village Road with Tee Hey Lane and is a finely constructed house of local stone which, over the mullioned window of its North wing carries a date stone carrying the attribution :

I.R.MR
I R JUNIOR 1668

This inscription, whilst giving the date of building, has generally been taken to mean that it was built by "JOHN ROBINSON JUNIOR" ("I" was frequently used in place of "J" at that time), but otherwise it has been regarded as problematic. It is most likely that the "MR" is the abbreviated form of MAJOR which was used in the 17th C to indicate an individual of a specified higher class, that is SENIOR as we would say today in relation to the older member of a family, usually the FATHER. From this we can conclude that the house was built as the home of:

JOHN ROBINSON SENIOR

(and)   JOHN ROBINSON JUNIOR

in 1668

who were most likely Father and Son.

Old Hall Farm and its barn

From its overall appearance and the quality of workmanship in the finely dressed stone and the well proportioned mullioned windows, this was no ordinary farm-house. It was definitely the house of someone of considerable means, and it has been suggested, though at present we have no direct evidence to support this, that it was the local Manor House. On the same basis it has been suggested that it was built on the site of an older Hall of the Bebington family. But by this time the Bebington family had died out and whilst it may have been built on the site of one of their halls this does not explain its rather grand form. In its later years on the South side of the front door there has been a glass covered verandah. It is scheduled as of Special Historical Interest.

For the greater part of the 19th C the house was occupied by the Oxton family, who had lived in the area for a long time before this and been land-owners. About the turn of the century the Johnsons farmed there. The land of the farm itself included that area now occupied by the Car-Showrooms on Tee Hey Lane and their car storage yard facing onto Village Road. One wonders whether it was a foretaste of its present day usage, but for some years, on this area when it was their farm-yard, Johnson had an old horse tram, one supposes one from the original Birkenhead tramways, that served as an outhouse and tool-shed. The farmyard had the usual out-buildings and a duck-pond. Their hay-bays and main stack-yard was on the Eastern side of Tee Hey Lane immediately opposite the farm, where the shops from the Post Office to Rowland Avenue are now. After the Johnsons, Howards worked the farm. They were there until just after WW2, when they moved to Cross Lane, and then in 1948 it was sold to the British Legion to become their Club Rooms.

On the corner of Tee Hey Lane and Village Road there used to be a gate to enter the property, not a good position with present day traffic, and it was closed off when the space at the side of the Hall was made into a car-park. Between this point and where there is the present entrance to the car-park, stood a large stone barn/granary. In 1964 this was demolished, primarily to make more parking space. The stone from it was used to face the extension to the Clubrooms that were built at the rear of the Hall. Many were disappointed that the stonework of the wall of this new extension was done in a 'Modern' style rather than in keeping with the traditional masonry of the Hall and that of the area

7

in general. The barn served other purposes than a granary. In the latter part of the 19th C there were many Irish labourers working in the quarries and at harvest times on the farms, but accommodation for them was not easy to find, so the barn was used as a dormitory for them. On Saturday nights they were the butt of much banter in the Inns and Ale houses in the village, and many of them woke sobered up to find themselves in the duck-pond at the back of the farm.

King's Yard and Broad Farm.

The area covered by the Co-op Stores on the corner of Town Lane and Tee Hey Lane was, until 1936, occupied by King's Yard which faced onto Town Lane, and a single house on the Tee Hey Lane corner. The house was generally known as Everard's, or even 'Granny Everard's', from the well known family who lived there. There was a wash-house at the back where Mrs Mary Everard, like many of the ladies in the village, took in washing to supplement their husband's wages. The washing came from the 'Big houses', not just those in the village, but Lower Bebington, Prenton, Tranmere and Oxton. It would have been really hard work; for a start the clothes would have been cotton or linen that had to be boiled and then washed in the dolly-tub with the 'peg', before rinsing, starching, drying and ironing, and all the water had to be fetched from the tap in the yard, the boiler fired and drying done whatever the weather. That was before the ironing started! "Old Blue" with his pony would collect and deliver the laundry to the 'Toffs' in Prenton.

The Everards were active with the local Methodist Church, one of the daughters taught in the Sunday School for very many years. They were also known further afield, for their son had a successful career in the Birkenhead Police Force.

He lived to be ninety two King's Yard at the top of Town Lane, was a court of six brick built, rendered and whitewashed cottages which stood on the Southern side of a cobbled yard, with a low stone wall on the Town Lane and Tee Hey Lane boundaries. The windows of the cottages were all made up of small diamond shaped panes in a cast-iron windowframe of overall Gothic shape, similar to those in the pair of cottages in Village Road opposite Mill Brow. The skill of casting such window frames is, I believe, all but lost; they occur in some churches and in recent years where replacement has been necessary, it has been found that even where an iron-founder was able and willing to do the work, the cost has been prohibitive. From the use of these type of windows and other points in their structure there have been suggestions that they were Alms Houses when originally built, but no evidence of this has been traced. Although they were named 'King's', they were of much earlier date, say, late 18th or very early 19th century, than when the King family, after whom roads and farms etc in the area are named, came to Bebington so this was most likely applied when they later came into the possession of that family .Along the Town Lane boundary on the Tee Hey Lane corner was a stone built slaughter-house,for the pigs that were kept in the row of styes at the bottom end of the property, and a brick built barn. Next there was an entry-way, before a pair of privies which, presumably, were for the use of all the residents at that time, although in later years there were toilets in their back yards. Right at the bottom end were the pig-styes, and a barn.

King's Yard about 1905

In his March 1874 report the Medical Officer of Health (Mr Samuel Spratly M.D.) commented particularly on the cleanliness of

Broad's Farm with its date tablet and fire mark

the privies. At that time the cottages only had surface drains from them, to a channel that ran to a grid in the centre of the yard. Mr Spratly seemed to feel that the general state of the property was good in comparison with that of many others in the area. He particularly commented on Mr Joseph Dabbs' cottage as being "in a most clean and hygenic condition, in fact it is a place that does credit to its owner." On a later visit, the slaughter house was open and in use, there were the carcases of six pigs hanging, and Mr Spratly was impressed by the cleanliness and absence of smell, but he did feel that as the premises were unlicenced and so close to the cottages, "The Board should look into the matter." .Next to Everard's, on Tee Hey Lane, was Broad's Farm. This was a severe, three storied brick-built Georgian house standing on a foundation platform of the local white sandstone. It carried a carved stone date-tablet with the initials: R and J.A 1752

Carved into the stone above the initials was a smiling face of the sun.It might be useful to explain the form of these date tablets, they occur widely on older properties, and have frequently been imitated on more recent buildings. The centre (usually upper) initial is that of the man's (husband's) surname, his Christian name initial to the left and his wife's Christian name initial to the right. Then the date when the house was built, below.

These are almost certainly the initials of John Ridgate and his wife, he was an elector in the district in 1727. Just below the date tablet was the Insurance Mark of the Sun Alliance Insurance Company, with the Ridgate's registered number as subscribers to the company.These plates showing the insignia of the company were used to identify which company was responsible for the property should a fire occur. Only the Firefighters from the company concerned would deal with the fire, employees of other companies would not take any action! Next to the farm were a couple of smaller, brick built cottages. One of these was a general grocery shop and in its later years was also the Post Office.

In the 1930's there was a considerable purge against properties which, it was felt, did not meet current living standards. The cottages were still without gas or electricity, and mains sewerage .Lighting was by oil lamps or candles, and cooking done on the fire-range. In spite of this, the families managed well; at least one of the ladies took in washing from the 'big houses' in the district to supplement her husband's

11

wages from the quarry.The houses were condemned in 1935 and, except for the barn at the Eastern end which remained until the Co-op was built in the 1950's, they were demolished 12 months later.Several well known families of the village were moved from here to Lower Bebington, or the Stanton and Brackenwood Estates.

2

Village Road

Although there are many who would say that Village Road in quite narrow, it is wider than it was up to about 1900. Then it was only a narrow lane that led up to the top part of the village and then, beyond what is now the School Lane junction, became Storeton Road leading to that village and the quarries. Pictures show it as having little or no metalling, really not much more than a farm track.

Victoria Hall

In Village Road, immediately above The Acorn, is Victoria Hall. As its name suggests it was built to commemorate Queen Victoria's Diamond Jubilee. The land was given by Catherine King and money sought by Public subscription for its construction. As in many schemes of this type, the amount subscribed fell short of needs, and it was offered to Christ Church, subject to their providing the necessary finance to complete the work, to be their Parish Hall. This would have been particularly appropriate, as we shall see later, with the land having been given by a member of the King family. However, as remains the case in similar circumstances even today, the Church could not meet the cost, so it was bought by the local Council who have retained it to this day. The Foundation Stone, by the side of the main door reads:

THIS STONE WAS LAID ON 22ND JUNE 1897
IN THE 61ST YEAR OF QUEEN VICTORIA'S REIGN
BY CATHERINE ELIZABETH KING OF OXTON
WHO GAVE THE LAND FOR THIS BUILDING

The Hall was opened by Mr W.E.Gladstone. He stayed the night with local digitaries, and was made an Honorary Member of the "Loyal

Order of Ancient Shepherds", Friendly Society. We shall see them later.

Victoria Hall and Village Road about 1910

When the Higher Bebington Urban District Board was set up in 1894, the Offices were at Victoria Hall. At the rear of the Hall was the 'Fire Reel Shed', and at various times there was much argument over the maintainance of this building which appears to have been part Board, part Private Enterprise responsibillity. It must have originally been the property of a man in the village, and he leased it in some way to the Board, for there are records of 'discussions' as to who should be responsible for repairs, and in particular, providing new doors, at one time. In the end it looks as if it was a case of 'meeting-half-way'. In its later life it was described not merely as the Fire Reel Shed, but as The Fire Station!

Just inside the porch of the Hall is a specimen of the Footprint bed that had been found in the quarries. The extension to the Hall was added after WW2 to give greater accommodation.

Higher Bebington Local Board

As we turn up Village Road, you will see that the boundary wall to the land on which Victoria Hall stands has been set back somewhat in order to improve vision for vehicles using the road in front of it. In this wall is the carved enblem of the Higher Bebington Local Board which was originally placed high on the wall of their Offices in King Street, Rock Ferry.

House in King Street, Rock Ferry that was the Higher Bebington Local Board Office of the late 19th Century

It is of credit to the then Town Clerk of the Borough of Bebington, the late Mr Gerald Chappell, that this was rescued when the properties were demolished in 1972. Unfortunately, however, it was upside down! When the wall was later being moved further back to its present position, several people drew attention to this and asked that it be reinstated the right way up. As you will see, in spite of their efforts, it is still upside down. As they say, some people don't know their armourials from their elbows. The initiative to set up Higher Bebington Local Board came in 1859, four years ahead of that of(Lower) Bebington.This was probably by virtue of its size, and the intiative of the business men who had come to live in Rock Park. An Election was held and the results were published on 2nd May 1859, by William Paton and Charles Jenkins, the Returning Officers.

There were ten members:
Thomas Fisher Redhead,of Rock Lane, described as 'Clerk in Orders', he was the Vicar of the recently built St Peter's Church in Rock Ferry.
Charles Hay Steele,Gentleman of Rock Ferry.
William Paton, Corn Merchant of Highfield, (it is interesting to note that he was also one of the Returning Officers).
William Stanley Harris, Paper Merchant of Highfield.
William Hampson, Farmer of Higher Bebington.
George Troughton, Clerk of Higher Bebington. (He, although the Vicar Designate of the new Church being built in Higher Bebington, is described merely as 'Clerk', not 'Clerk in Orders').
William Huntriss, Hotel Keeper of Rock Ferry.
Philip Henry Chambres, Cotton Broker of The Dell, Rock Ferry.
Richard Nicholson, Merchant of Highfield.
George Comer, Cotton Merchant of Rock Park.
James Trevelyan Raynes, Broker of Rock Park.
William Thomas Hamilton, Surgeon of Rock Lane.

The first Meeting was held at The Royal Rock Hotel, in the evening of Monday 9th May 1859, all the elected members were present. They each made and signed the required Statutory Declaration as to their respective qualifications, these are the ones given in the above list. The Revd Thomas Fisher Redhead was appointed Chairman for the ensuing year, on the proposal of Mr Dobson, seconded by Mr Nicholson. "For the present", it was agreed that the Offices of the Board should be at Mr Robert Dobson's, at 9 King Street, Rock Ferry.This raises the question, "Who was this Mr Dobson?". He is not on the list of elected members. In the directory of the time, Mr Dobson is described as Estate Agent and Assistant Overseer, and 'R&J Dobson' are cited as Joiners and Builders in Rock Ferry. That is all we know of him. It was agreed that a proper Seal should be provided for the Board, and Mr Raynes designed this. As far as we know, this was the same as the carved stone Emblem that was placed in the wall above Mr Dobson's Offices, and is now in the wall outside Victoria Hall, in Village Road.

Houses and Shops.

Leaving Victoria Hall, the first cottage will be remembered until the late 1950's as Mrs Davis' greengrocers, a typical small village shop based on an ordinary house, selling fresh fruit and vegetables to the local people. Next above is a pair of cottages built of finely dressed local stone, these have been well cared for and, particularly early in the year when their wisteria is in flower they are the epitome of the 'country cottage'. Just above the second cottage is a way to the rear of that cottage; when the Bradshaw's lived there they had a Nursery behind the house and used to sell roses, flowers not the plants. One lady in the village used to make wreathes and it was from the Bradshaws that she liked to get her flowers.

There is now an open space before the entrance which goes to where the bowling green was behind The Royal Oak, that is used as their car park. Here, until the mid 1930's were three cottages, the background to their demolition is an important commentary on the social conditions of the day, so we will digress for a moment to explain the situation. Whereas today, if property does not meet present requirements, it is usually possible to obtain grants to remedy the deficiencies. At that time there was the general view that any properties that were not up to standard should be demolished. In fact, under an Act of 1930, a grant was given when this was carried out. Virtually all the properties in villages like this, and even in larger towns, was rented, so many landlords saw in this a means of getting rid of some of their liabilities and making some money at the same time. This was the fate of many cottages in the area which today would have been restored with great care, or maybe even had Preservation Orders served on them as being of special interest.

The first cottage, which stood back somewhat and had been built in 1621, was really small, single storey with a thatched roof. It housed Mr Harry Smith; he was not a Firbob, he came from New Ferry, and carried on his cobbler's business from the cottage. He had a painted sign board at the side of his door giving his name and profession. When the cottage was demolished he moved to a shop further up the road, as we shall see. Next were a pair of two storey semi-detatched cottages of well dressed stone, bearing a date- tablet for 1840 and the initials E and T. W. These most probably replaced a pair of earlier ones similar to Harry Smith's. We are not sure who built them but it could have been Waring, as the Waring family lived in one of them in the latter part of 19th C; Mr Waring was a tin-smith and they also sold milk,—a strange combination of trades, and no explanation as to where their milk came from! All three of these cottages were part of the Royal Oak parcel of property, belonging to the King family. In July and August of 1877 , there was an outbreak of Typhoid fever which affected them and the Corfe family at the Royal Oak. The Medical Officer Of Health stopped them selling the milk to try to contain the outbrake,— it is not on record that he stopped the sale of beer at the Royal Oak, though!

Harry Smith, the cobbler at the door of his cottage

The Royal Oak.

This Inn is beautifully constructed of local white stone laid in regular courses, each stone being finely worked down. The date tablet over the door shows that it was built in 1739, but we can only guess that the name of its first occupants was Taylor from the initials on the date tablet, as the records of the property do not go that far back. From the quality of workmanship in its construction and its proportions, it seems most unlikely that it was originally built to be an alehouse. This, together with the initialled date stone would suggest it being the home of a yeoman farmer. When it became an Inn we do not know, a reasonable guess would suggest the early part of the 1800's. Throughout its history it was always only a beer-house, and never sold wines or spirits.

In 1880 the property "All that piece or parcel of land with the Public House called or known as the "ROYAL OAK" and four cottages erected thereon—-" was sold by the Trustees of the late Catherine King, who had died in 1878, to the Birkenhead Brewery Company Ltd. The land included that on which Mersey View now stands; this was sold for development in early 1882.

The cottages mentioned were the three immediately below the Inn and one which was roughly where No 1 Mersey View now stands. From the mid-part of the last century until 1898, the licence was held by Martha Corfe, and the notice over the door stated that she was licenced 'to sell Ale, Beer and Porter'. Although only a beer house, it could, at the turn of the century, offer beds for two travellers, it had one stable with two stalls but could offer no refreshments, sounds like bed-without-breakfast.

The terrace houses on the opposite side of the road were not built until about 1905, so there was a clear line of sight up to The George. The story is told, by several of the older Fir-Bobs, that in her later years, Mrs Corfe had difficulty getting about and walked with a stick. Much of her time she then spent in her upstairs room with the window that looks out to the front. If she saw a man leaving "The George" and making his way as if to come to the "Royal Oak", she would rap on the floor with her stick as a sign that the next man in had been to "The George" and was not to be served, such was the rivalry. In common with other Inns, prior to the introduction of 'Restricted Hours' by the Licencing Laws of 1914, it has been recollected seeing men on their way to work, waiting outside the Inn at times between 6.00 and 7.00 am to have a drink before starting the day.

"The Royal Oak" with members of the Corfe family in the late 19th century

Over the years there have been many landlords. When age and failing health forced Martha Corfe to retire, the licence passed to James Corfe on 25th May 1898. Fred Browning followed James Corfe, with Fred Hayes in the 1930's, Les Manson, Douglas Cameron Grant and finally J.Howarth who provided free beer in large enamel jugs on the last night before the Inn closed for the last time, on 5th May 1960, to be replaced by The Acorn in the centre of the village. This naming certainly parodies the old saying for here we have "a mighty 'Acorn' from a tiny 'Royal Oak' hath grown"!

It was well patronised as a meeting place by the men of the village, and many of their social clubs met there. Several of these carried out Charitable work both locally and, particularly during the last war, nationally. These received active support from local dignitaries including Aldermen of the Borough and the then Town Clerk.There was a bowling green at the back on which many a happy hour could be spent, this was greatly missed when the Inn closed.

Following its closure as an Inn the house became the offices of the architects, Paterson Macauley and Owen, who were responsible for the design of the Bebington Civic Centre, and many other public buildings. More recently an advertising agency, Austin Stirrup, have set up their offices there.

Sergeant Charles Ewart

While we are in this area, there is one person who is reported to have lived in a cottage about here who should be mentioned. This was Sergeant Charles Ewart of the North British Dragoon Guards (now the Scots Greys).

First, the story of the man, and then what we believe to be his association with the village. Ewart was born at Beddoes' Farm, Elvanfoot in 1769. When he was 20 he enlisted in the army at Kilmarnock, became a proficient swordsman and was Fencing Master of his regiment. After serving in the 1793-5 campaigns he became a Sergeant serving in Captain Vernor's troop at Waterloo. It was here that he captured a French Regimental Eagle Standard: this brought him fame and recognition, and the Eagle was adopted for his Regimental Badge. In 1816 he was given an Ensign Lieutenent's commision in the 5th Veterans' Battalion, and when this was disbanded in 1821 he was retired on full pay of 5 shillings and 10 pence a day. His later years were spent, with his wife, in Davyhulme, Manchester, where he died on 23rd March 1846 aged 77. He was buried in the Swedenborgian Cemetery there, which by the 1930's had become a builder's yard. In August 1936 his grave was 'discovered' and he was reinterred with full military honours by the Scots Greys on the Esplanade at Edinburgh Castle in May 1938.

Sergeant Ewart capturing the French Standard. (Ryall's engraving of Ansdell's painting, "The Fight For The Standard")

As with many such outstanding events of that time, a graphic painting of the incident at Waterloo was made, by the artist Ansdell, and prints from an engraving based on this by Ryall were published. In 1954 a framed copy of this engraving was given to Bebington Library as being of particular local interest. This was stated by the donor to be because Ensign Ewart had, before leaving to live in Davyhulme, "—for a time, lived in Higher Bebington, in a cottage adjacent to the Royal Oak Inn ", or, "—returned (after Waterloo) to a cottage immediately next to the Royal Oak". It was also stated that the local residents subscribed to give him an engraved silver watch. Unfortunately, the actual notes the donor gave cannot be traced, and he died some years ago. Efforts by the author and others have, so far, failed to obtain clarification of these points, but we believe that the donor had some reliable evidence for these statements and our searches continue. So, for the present, all we can say is that there is a strong possibility that Ewart lived for a while in one of the cottages that used to be close to the Royal Oak in Village Road.

Mersey View

The land immediatly above the Royal Oak was sold for development, the single cottage that faced the road demolished and Mersey View, a row of 13 terrace houses, built early in 1882. By making this terrace 'end-on' to the road, the land was used to good advantage and gave the houses a pleasant prospect which makes them attractive even by today's standards. Although at the back they only have a small yard and an entry-way, they have, for their time, good little front gardens with a path at the ends of them to the road.

The Chap-Man

The group of shops on the other side of Village Road between Sandfield Road and Victoria Road are quite modern. Before they were built this was, perpetuated in the road name, a sand-field area. It was here that each Friday the travelling 'Chap-man', Fred Bell set up his stall. He was known variously as 'Cheap-Jack', with no reflections on the quality of his wares, or 'Ding-Dong' from punning on his name, and his ringing of a bell to announce his arrival. He had begun his working life about 1900 as a 10 year old on a milk round in Birkenhead, earning 1shilling and tuppence a week. About the beginning of WW1 he started his own business as a Chandler and then, after serving 3 years in Mesopotamia, he returned to begin his rounds with a horse and van selling hardwear and domestic products. Children would be eager to 'help' him, to get the reward of a ride on the horse's back to his next stop in the village. He also called at the end of School Lane and then on to Prospect Hill. Here his main sales were of paraffin, as there was no gas or electric laid-on for heating, cooking or lighting. By 1927 he set up with a motor van to cover more ground, visiting houses and farms all over Wirral, not giving up full-time work until he was 75 years old. He then took a part-time job until he was 80!

More Businesses

Above Mersey View are a pair of houses that have served as shops of several types over the years. The first one (No 24), now a private house was, in the early part of the 20th C, Ernie Williams' greengrocery shop.

His advertisement in the Parish Magazines in 1912 describes his business as "Fruiterer, Greengrocer and Market Gardener, -Orders Delivered Daily". He had a horse and cart for this, and to do a mobile business in the district. Later, the fish and chip shop that had been further up the road moved here, and continued for a long time. Finally, it was used by Noel Lacey as part of his car repair/servicing business that was more or less to the rear of the shop, to sell spare parts and accessories for cars.

The next shop, now an Insurance Agency, is remembered by all as Sam Ledsome's, the cobblers. When Harry Smith's cottage was demolished it was vacant, and he moved his cobbler's business here. When he gave up, Mr Ledsome took over the business. Sam was a great character of the village, greatly missed by those who knew him, not just for his helpful ways as a cobbler and repair man for all those annoying little jobs in leather that he could do 'while you waited', but for himself, as a friend. There was always a smile and a cheery 'Hello' when you called in the shop,—even as you passed by. His outlook on life was well summed up in the framed "Motto" he had on his shop wall, "I used to grumble because I had no shoes, until the other day

Looking down Village Road about 1890, with two shops, the first of which later became Harry Smith the Cobbler's followed by Sam Ledsome, the lower one was Williams'green grocery. Then there is Mersey view and "The Royal Oak". Note there were no houses on the Southern side of the road at that time.

when I met a man who had no feet". Prior to this, it was Mr George Trantom's grocery shop which he had moved from higher up the road, on the other side.

It is at this point that King's Brow deviates from Village Road, and alongside Sam Ledsome's shop a driveway goes to the yard area at the back, now accommodating a motor repairer's and other businesses. The house immediately above this on the right on King's Brow is detached, and was built by Jack Lee the village contractor, early in 1882 for his family, and the yard then gave ample space for his equipment and supplies. On a photograph taken soon after this, quite a large crane can be seen stretching its jib above the roof. His work covered a wide area, not just Bebington; he built the house of a lady I knew in Bromborough. The sign board outside his house read;

John Lee & Son,
General Contractor,
Horticultural Builders,
Hot Water Engineers,
All Jobbing Practically Attended To.

The statement of being 'Hot Water Engineers' had some positive backing. Not only did they instal water heating equipment, they designed it, too. In the Liverpool Directory for 1892, it states that they were:

Patentees for the Bebington Boiler, as supplied to Her Majesty's
Government.

That is some achievement for a contractor in a small village like ours As well as being a builder, he had a very extensive orchard, that stretched from the back of his house to Well Lane, -hence the naming of the cul-de-sac off Well Lane as Orchard Way. Of course, such an orchard was a great temptation to all the boys, and quite a few of the girls, in the village who, naturally enough went to great lengths to avoid being caught there and invoking his wrath. But, come the time when the fruit was ready he would have a good sized basket of apples by his front gate and as the children passed on their way to school they could take one (or two!). He sold the apples, a basketful for 6d, if you

King's Brow, with John Lee's and Peers' Brothers' signs in front of their houses.

went to the orchard in Well Lane. The quality of his fruit was such that he frequently entered his apples in Shows in Liverpool.

The Village Smith

Let's just look at this end of King's Brow. This is quite steep, to the extent that in our present 'cared-for' age a hand rail has been put there. So, it is perhaps a little surprising that the top house with the out-building above which is now its garage, was the house and forge of the local Smith, Jos Peers. His brother, William, was the wheelwright who used the field on which the school now stands to do the tyring of large wheels. They worked as;

Peers Bros.,
Coach Builders, Wheelwrights,
Forging and Shoeing.

Jos Peers, who had left school in 1882 'To go into Trade', had a high reputation as a smith; many of the contract masons working at the quarries would take their tools to him rather than the quarry smith for reconditioning, hardening and tempering. On frosty mornings, particularly if there had been a fall of snow, there would be a queue of horses up the Brow waiting to be 'Spiked', - that is, have chisel shaped pieces of iron inserted in the small square holes of their shoes, to stop them slipping on the roads. There was only room for one horse at a time in the forge. The children of the village would often take a potato to roast in his hearth on the cold wintery days, as well. Jos's talents also extended to singing in the Church Choir. Of his family, one son, Stephen was successful in business and became an Alderman and Mayor of Ellesmere Port.

King's Brow

On the triangle of land formed by King's Brow and Village Road were other cottages. At the top, were two small, two storey ones, and on the side facing Village Road, a long, low thatched cottage which became known as 'Mercer's Cottage' from the family who lived there. They were related to Joe Mercer, the footballer who was born in Ellesmere Port. Built into the stone wall of this plot, facing Village Road, was a

Mercer's cottage and the little chip shop just above it, about 1880.

very small shop,'The Hole In The Wall', which at various times sold sweets, tobacco and newspapers, and later Mrs Joynson sold fish and chips from there before moving to the shop lower down that we have already mentioned.

As the road levels off slightly at the top end of this triangle there is, on the right, a pair of low, single storey cottages, probably built in the latter part of 18th C. They are of rough stone, rendered with pebble-dash and have very attractive, small windows with diamond shaped panes set in cast iron frames. The low construction of these cottages typifies the efforts to keep buildings out of the wind in these exposed areas, by keeping their roof-line below that of the crest of the hill. Like so many other cottages in the village that had the space, there were pig-styes at the back of them.

The middle part of Village Road in the early 1900's. Mr Fred Hancock outside his shop, and the Post Office next door-but-one with its Bell Telephone sign.

Terrace Houses and Shops.

Now let's turn round and look from this point at the terrace houses that were built on the Southern side in about 1900. Almost opposite the cottages we have just looked at is the triangular shaped end of the row and this house, No 47A was designed as a shop. At first it was occupied by Mr Fred Hancock, a butcher who came from Neston. Of all his trade, it seems his Black Puddings and Brawn bring back the most treasured memories. In fact his advertisments specifically listed "Corned Beef, Pickled Tounges, Black Puddings and Brawn".

Next one down the road,No 47, George Trantom's grocery,and as his advertisement in the Parish Magazine said,-

GEO. TRANTOM

Higher Bebington Village Grocer,

Tea Specialist, Bacon and Butter Expert,

Trantom's Delicious Breakfast Bacon tempts the Poorest Appetite.

After a while he moved lower down the road to No 26. As the shop he left offered more room, Mr Hancock moved in from his smaller one on the end. His son, Tommy, took over and is still well remembered in the village. For many years, Woods' Newsagents was at No 45 that in its earlier years had been the Post Office, until they moved to the newer shop on the corner of Victoria Road. As the Post Office has been in several places over the years, we will look at that separately.

"The George Hotel".

We need to go back to the early part of the 19th century to look at the beginnings of The George Hotel. In talking of Old Hall Farm we said that the Oxtons were there certainly in the mid 1800's. A son of the family, John married a Miss Johnson who had some finances of her own, and she saw a business opportunity in providing 'refreshment' for the quarrymen close to their work. She bought a cottage on Prospect Hill and set up a Beer House. John Oxton's family were not without experience in this field. An antecedent of his, another John Oxton who had married Jane Goldborne, " a widow of Tranmere", on 12th September 1655 was "a Husbandman at Storeton, (who) also brewed and had a beer-house".

His wife's venture proved successful, providing her not only with an income but enabling her to build up some capital reserve. They used this to buy cottages, probably three though it may have been four, opposite the end of Mill Road, between Mill Brow and what is now School Lane. The lower one of these they made into a beer-house and, as it backed more or less directly onto the mill that had been quite newly erected by Mr Lightbound, they obtained a licence for it on 11th October 1838 under the name of "The Windmill". The renewal licence they obtained in 1841 is still retained by a descendent of the family who lives in the village. Two of the other cottages they made into a bakery, and this too was a successful business. Their bread was delivered as far as the cottages in Thornton Hough, and at Brimstage to the Inn, 'The Red Cat' which stood on what is now a village green and has a childrens nursery centre standing on it.

Thomas Oxton and his wife, Mary, took over the licence of The Windmll on his father's death.Somewhere in the mid 1800's the lower cottage was demolished and a substantial inn in the Georgian style built in its place which, naturally enough was then named 'The George Hotel'.The bakery at the other two cottages continued in business until they were demolished in 1936. The Hotel is on record as providing 'Good accommodation' and being able to supply refreshments for 50 people. It also had 'two beds for travellers, and there is one stable with three stalls'. Apart from the main entrance there was a 'side door' at the top end of the property for 'Off-sales'.

Thomas Oxton died in 1890 and the property passed to his sister, Mrs Jane Barnett, and although it had always been a 'Free-house' and later returned to being one, it was leased to Bent's Brewery in 1896 for about 10 years,and Elizabeth Mary Fox was brought in as Licencee.

A rather strange point that we have not been able to clarify is apparent in the Deeds. In 1912 a mortgage was obtained on the Inn; this would be quite a normal thing to occur in order to raise capital for business puposes but in this instance, the mortgage was held by The University of Wales. Why this was so we have not been able to find out, but it does seem strange that such an institution should have an interest in an Hotel in such a small village. Later, the Hotel was owned by Mrs Barnett's daughter, Mrs Mary Ellis. It then became known as 'Ellis's George Hotel', and this name appears on the sign board of the time.

"The George" in the late 1800's from a watercolour by Weville

"The George" as rebuilt in the 1930's

It is strange that the story told by some older Fir-Bobs of Mrs Corfe at 'The Royal Oak' sitting at an upstairs window and signalling by knocking on the floor with her stick that the next man in had just been to 'The George' and was not to be served, is also told by other, knowledgable Fir-Bobs, 'in reverse', that Mrs Ellis did the same thing! Most likely, there is some truth in both if there was that sort of rivallry. Again, as at the' Royal Oak', in the time before there were restricted hours, men would call in "The George" for a pint at about 7 am before going to work at the quarries, the new soap works at Port Sunlight or the ship-building yards in Birkenhead. In the evenings their wives would call in to the Off-sales for a jug of ale for them.

In 1926 Mrs Ellis sold the Hotel to The West Cheshire Brewery who, in 1936 rebuilt it in its present form. Throughout its history, the licence of this Inn/Hotel was held in the same family for over a hundred years. The new "George" was built in the modern style of the 1930's, the particularly interesting feature though is that it presents the same design on both the Northern and Southern sides. This was done assuming that Tee Hey Close as it is now called was going to be continued to meet Village Road at the point where there is the Hotel car park; the Hotel would then have presented a similar aspect to both Village Road and this new road. The advent of WW2 stopped this being done and the effect is rarely appreciated. In more recent years, though it has remained little changed on the outside, there have been changes internally to keep up with changes in use of these type of establishments. A few years ago, when this was done it was decided to give it a more 'Contemporary' name to attract the younger clientel, and it was called 'The Tutt and Shive'. However, in 1998 its original name of 'The George' with an attractive portrait sign-board was restored.

3

Mill Road

Probably to all but the younger generation, and perhaps even to them, through hearing their family talk, the Mill Road Schools are still spoken of as The New Schools, after more than 80 years. They were built by Jack Lee, the village contractor in 1913. Prior to this, William Peers had used the field, with a large stable that stood there, when doing his wheelwrighting, particularly when shrinking-on the iron tyres to the wheels.

Holly Hall Cottage

Immediately opposite the schools is the top of King's Brow, and on its Northerly corner is No 18 Mill Road, the first of a row of six pairs of semi-detached houses built in the 1930's. Attached to the side of the house is a garage, erected by the present owners. When they were preparing the ground to lay the concrete foundation slab for this they had some difficulty when they reached an area covered with closely, regularly packed, rounded pebbles each about 4-5 inches across. It was not until quite a long time later when they saw a picture of Holly Hall Cottage which had stood at the corner of King's Brow and Mill Road that they realised that this area had been the carefully cobbled footpath in front of the King's Brow side of the cottage, and was still there under a foot or so of soil. Holly Hall cottage was built in 1394, and was of cruck construction. This method of building, which originated in the 14th century or slightly earlier, was to set up a pair of curved timbers obtained by cutting down the length of a single, slightly curved tree to give a pair of "legs" with a cross tie about ⅔ the height, to form an 'A' frame to support the ridge-pole. There were usually three such pairs of timbers to a cottage, though further pairs were often added,

35

"Holly Hall Cottage" at the top of King's Brow with its cobbled pavement

The interior of" Holly Hall Cottage" from a water colour

some at a later date, to provide extra 'bays'. In the earlier forms, wattle and daub walls were built but later these were superseded (replaced in existing structures) by stone or brick walls up to the eaves. The roof was thatched and came down to where the cross-brace fitted onto the crucks. The fireplace, generally a massive structure in a stone chimney-piece, was set in an end wall. To protect from draughts a wall was built between the doorway in the side wall and the fireplace. A round hole in this wall at eye level, called a 'speer', enabled the residents to see who was at the door. A settle often backed onto this wall, or was built onto it, to provide a fireside seat. On the back of the wall would be pegs of cow, ram or deer horn to hang coats and hats on. Pictures of the interior of Holly Hall in 1880 show it with a 'Modern' cast-iron cooking range, with a wooden 'warming cupboard' at the side, in which the bread dough could be put to 'rise'. Such cupboards, which could be quite large, have often been mistakenly described as Priest-holes. In its later years, a wash-house with a corrugated iron roof was added to the Western end of the cottage, as the tenant was one of the many ladies who did washing for the 'Big houses' in the district. Holly Hall, like so many of other cottages, was scheduled for demolition in the 1930's. There was strong and protracted opposition to this from many Councillors and members of The Bromborough Society on the grounds of its historical and architectural importance. All to no avail, and in 1934 it was pulled down. Such was the strength of feeling that in the edition of the Birkenhead News in which this was reported, the date of the paper was given as 1394 , the year that the cottage was built, rather than 1934! Some of the residents in the then newly built semi-detached houses remember having their peace rudely shattered on occasions in WW2 by the anti-aircraft guns which the thoughtful Ministry of Defence had sited on the field opposite, now Mill Butt Close.

Other Cottages.

Immediately beyond the semi-detached houses is No 32, a two storey, rendered, stone built house set end-on to the road. Although in its present form it may not attract more than passing notice, it holds considerable interest for the historian. Photographs, probably taken in the latter part of the 19th century, though not readily dated, show it as a stone built, single storey cottage, with a massive chimney in the end wall by the road. Even in the 1960's non of the older people in the village could recollect it in that form, so we have not been able to decide when it was altered. Its general form in that picture suggests that it was, like Holly Hall, of cruck construction, so it too was probably built in the 15th century, if not earlier. Although we have not been able to find out when it was modified to its present form, it recently had the rendering removed for renewal, and this revealed the form of the modifications. The ground floor was indeed built of stone, and it was possible to identify some of the individual stonework in it from the old photograph. The upper floor had been constructed of brickwork, and the modifications to the doorway and windows could be traced. We should add that it does not have, nor ever has had, a date tablet as has been stated by some authors, this error arises from confusion with another cottage on the other side of the road.

No 32 Mill Road as it is today.

Opposite to the cottage, where No 35 now stands, there were until the 1930's two small stone cottages. Next is a pair of very stately vil-

No.32 Mill Lane as it was until the latter part of the 19th century

las built in the late 18th C originally called 'Rock Mount' and 'Clyde Villa'. These are being maintained well and represent a good example of this type of housing of that time.

Mill Butt Farm

Next to these, separated by an entrance-way, is Mill Butt House or, more correctly, Mill Butt Farm, now a private house. Originally it was a dairy farm, but also carried a good stock of pigs. Its land extended over most of the area between Mill Road and Mount Road from the top of Well Lane to where the present school stands. Its name lends evidence to the view that the original, or at least one of the earlier, Higher Bebington mills stood on or very close to its lands. Today, the main house with its outbuildings and a yard remain. Many parts of the house have been extensively altered over the years. In its present form it probably dates from the late 18th, or early 19th century. As is usual, the deeds do not record sufficient early detail to trace back beyond the latter half of the 19th C. During recent alterations a well was found in one of the front rooms and this, together with other structural points, confirm that the present frontage was added to an earlier building. During the latter part of its life as a farm it was tenanted by Mr John (Joggler) Joynson, and on his death it passed to his son, Barney. For the greater part of the 19th C it was owned, like much property in the area, by members of the King family, and was subject to many complex Settlements. It is intriguing that one of the Trustees in these Settlements was The Reverend William Archibald Spooner, Warden of New College, Oxford, renowned for his (legendary) verbal eccentricities,- "Spoonerisms". He had married a grand daughter, Frances Wycliffe Goodwin, of George King of Higher Bebington Hall.

Almost opposite Mill Butt Farm now stands a most imposing modern house, No 38, built in 1976. This house stands on what was the garden of the Southern one of the pair of houses just round the corner from Well Lane in Mill Road. These may have originally have been a single house, 'Claremont', most likely built at the end of the 18th or early in the 19th century. The greater part of the garden of this house was on its Southern side, along Mill Road, and had a high wall constructed of local stone in the traditional form to keep it private; the

1932 Season ticket for 'Claremont Cinema'

wall, but of considerably reduced height, has been retained. As the wall stood originally, there was a boarded extension on top some two feet high, and then a slightly sloping, boarded roof. This was generally dismissed as being a long, lean-to garden shed or conservatory by those passing along the road. Actually this timberwork was built by the owners son in the 1930's to house a private cinema. At the time, Mr Quigley lived there, and his son (Sonny) and friends fitted up the interior with two Pathe 16 mm projectors, a radiogramophone, and easy chairs to accommodate up to about twenty people. They could then give film shows to the family, friends and Father's business associates. It is only within the last couple of years one of Sonny's friends, who helped with this, found the wiring diagrams he had drawn out at the time for the lighting to give fading effects to the different parts of the 'Theatre'.

Inglefield Cottage

It is the cottage opposite the top of Well Lane which carries the date tablet for 1720 that has been confused with No 32, we mentioned earlier. This tablet has the initials E and F, I, being those of Ernest Inglefield and his wife, Florence and the cottage is generally called Inglefield Cottage. This cottage, like No 32, is end-on to the road. At one time it was a 'tied cottage' to Mill Butt Farm, which further suggests that the farm dates back quite some time. Inglefield cottage is shorter than it was, the Eastern end protruded nearly 10 feet further into the road than now. This was accommodated by a distinct 'Dog-leg' in Mill Road where it passed the top of Well Lane. But it was decided that this had to be realigned to smooth traffic flow. Following lengthy negotiations with the owner, the authorities undertook the removal of the "offending" length. This was done by first carefully numbering and indexing all the stones that made up the end wall. These were then removed and stored while the necessary shortening was effected. The 'new' end wall was then built with the original stones in the same juxtapositions as in the original wall. Whilst the wall was being taken down, the interior fireplace and chimney was removed to be put in the new position in the house. As this chimney was dismantled, it revealed the well worn hand and foot holds that had been used by sweeps boys in cleaning the chimney over the years. It is only when we see evidence like this that we accept the reality of the jobs these children had to do.

At the same time that this was done, a large solidly built stone barn belonging to the cottage, that stood on a triangular island of land at the junction of Well Lane and Mill Road was also demolished, and the whole level and gradients of the junction altered to suit modern traffic. There was, on this island, a well, which was most likely the one from which Well Lane took its name. They were very careful to re-erect the massive retaining walls on both sides of the top of Well Lane in the traditional style, a really attractive feature.

Apart from the loss of part of this lovely old cottage, although it was most thoughtfully carried out, it is perhaps a little disappointing that in an area so famed for its high quality building stone and walling craftsmen, that the garden wall of the cottage was replaced with one of precast- concrete blocks. There used to be a lovely "Old English Garden" to the cottage, but much of this was lost when the house was shortened, and it has been further decreased by the needs of vehicle access. The house itself, apart from the 'restored' end wall, has been cement rendered and painted, obliterating the finely cut, finished and laid stone blocks from which it was built. The lady who lived there at the time was very proud of the garden, and also excelled in making the most delightfully dressed dolls.

Well Lane

Let's just look down Well Lane while we are here. As we have said, Jack Lee's orchards were on the South side and were well patronised. On the North side, where the modern detached houses (Nos 8-20) stand was a delph left by a minor quarrying venture. Some stone, mostly of walling rather than building quality, was taken from here, but with there being much of the softer yellow stone it was mainly worked for sand. Following WW1, John Williams (Snr) who lived on Mill Terrace, established a Nursery here. He was a general market gardener and florist, with greenhouses as well as the open cultivated area. He sold herbaceous and bedding plants, and cut flowers. These were available until only a few tears before the present houses were built after WW2.

Some 'Big Houses'.

It is interesting to note that the more Northern part of Mill Road, beyond the top of Well Lane, used to be regarded as part of, and was called, Well Lane. Before it was finally decided that it was more logical to see it as a continuation of Mill Road, it was also called Mill Well Lane; this name appears on many legal documents up to the early part of the 20th C. A little further along Mill Road on the Northern side we come to the cul-de-sac of Heather Bank, the building of which was started in the mid-1930's by Tom Owen, who lived in one of the houses he had built on Mount Road. WW2 meant that he did not complete the estate to include the six houses on Mill Road until 1955. The estate was originally the site of a large villa called "Heather Bank"; the house stood near the top of the present road, with its main entrance from Mount Road. Along the Mill Road boundary was a stone wall of fair sized blocks, and just inside this was a row of stately beech trees. The house was built for Mr Donald Kendall who had a printing and stationery business, and his family towards the end of the 19th century; prior to this they had lived in a smaller house further along Mount Road. One of Mr Kendall's hobbies was watercolour painting, and several people in the village have examples of his work. Prior to being developed for houses, Mr Coombes, who lived in Village Road, had a rose nursery on this area.

On the Eastern side of Mill Road, just before it turns up to Mount Road, was "Bentfield", originally built for a Mr Moses who was a restaurateur in Old Hall Street in Liverpool. Later Mr Perkins lived there, he had a millinery business under the name of Madame de Jong. Its last owners were the Hardings, and when Mrs Harding died it was sold for housing development. There were good gardens, with banks of rhododendrons along its Mill Road frontage, and about 5 acres of field going down to King's Road. On this were built Bentfield Gardens and Bentfield Close, in 1957.

Bentfield was a fine house, of rich red brick, well proportioned and had a glass cupola on the roof that gave fine views over the whole of Liverpool and the Mersey from Widnes to the Bar. When it was being demolished I talked with the contractor. He told me that in his business there was no real room for sentiment but it made him feel uncomfortable pulling that house down as it was so well made, the windows were all of ¼inch bevelled plate glass, and he could see no evidence of rot or woodworm that is usually common in such houses of that age.

To the South of the Bentfield estate is "Rotherwood", an estate of modern detached houses. The house which stood here was in its later years divided into flats, but had originally been built slightly earlier than 'Bentfield' for Mr Alfred Higgins, and later owned by Mr J.Brooks Poole. In the early part of the 20th C, Mr Kirkland-Mole, or as spelt in some Directories of the day, Mr Keartland-Mole, a fruit importer in Castle Street in Liverpool lived there. These are just three typical examples of the 'Big houses' that were built in Higher Bebington in the latter part of the 19th century by merchants and business men seeking more rural surroundings.

'Bentfield' looking over to the church

4

The Wind-Mill

Wirral is an area that has been rich in mills, though many have unfortunately disappeared. Being fairly exposed to the Westerly winds, even in quite low-lying sites mills have operated successfully. The rapidity with which the sails and caps of those on the more exposed positions have been damaged or destroyed even when cared for in their working life is ample evidence of the the powers that were utilised to provide flour for the daily bread. However, we do need to be careful in talking to some of the older Gentlemen in the village about Higher Bebington mill.

"Oh yes," they will say, "you know that there used to be two wind-mills,don't you?"

"No, I thought there was only one" you reply.

Whereupon it is explained to you "Well, that is because they had to pull one of them down."

"Oh, why?" you ask.

"Well, you see," it is explained very seriously, "there wasn't enough wind for both of them!"

That is what you get from Fir-Bobs!

The ideality of the ridge between Higher Bebington and Storeton as a site for a wind-mill had been realised from early times. There is documentary evidence of a mill in the mid 13th C, and as far back as 1424 Thomas Hough is recorded as being the miller, though we do not know just where the mill stood.The presence of a mill is recorded in Elizabeth 1 days; no description of the mill has been traced, beyond it being of the post type. Again, where it stood is not clear; some evidence suggests that it was in the area just to the North of where 'The Travellers' Rest' stands, perhaps on what is now the school playing field. The next really firm evidence of the mill is in 1768 when William Lightbound, of Bromborough mill who was the leasee of Higher Bebington mill (most likely from the Stanleys of Storeton) died and bequeathed this mill to his son Samuel. A Rebecca Lightbound's maiden name was Hough, the name of the miller in 15th century, this suggests that the mill had been worked by the same family throughout this time and then, by marriage continued to be a 'family' concern. Samuel died in 1798, the mill passed to his son, Thomas. In his Will, William Lightbound also left Willaston and Tranmere mills to two other sons.

There is also conflicting evidence of where this mill stood. In 1827 it was rebuilt in brick as a 5 storey smock mill, the mill we have known. On a map which predates this by only a few years, the mill is shown as being on the Southwestern corner of Rest Hill and Mount Road, and does not show any other mill in the area. However, Greenwood's map of 1819, 8 years before the rebuilding, shows it where it was rebuilt in 1827, and where we have always seen it. We know this, and that the Millwright was A.Ball, as he left his mark and the date on one of the beams in the mill. Later in the 19th century Lightbounds rented the mill to Samuel Johnson, who later obtained the freehold. He left the mill to his son, Harry, who continued working it until about 1909. He retained the property until it was bought by Williams, the builders in 1947. Its end came when it was demolished in 1968 by another building firm who had acquired it two years earlier.

In its heyday the mill was an impressive sight. Massive sails with the cap that turned to take full advantage of the wind, a gallery round it for access to the sails and kept freshly whitewashed each Whit Monday. On its third floor were five pairs of stones, fed by hoppers on the upper floors.

Harry Johnson complained when he was young that his father called him at all hours to get the sails set right when the wind blew up.The sails (sweeps) of the mill were timber frames, with heavy cotton cloth over them to catch the wind, and the amount of cloth sail on each sweep had to be adjusted according to the wind strength, and balanced for each sweep. This was a skilled job, and depending on the weather, could be arduous and not without danger. At intervals, usually each year, but if conditions had been severe, more frequently, the cloth for the sails had to be renewed. When this was done there was much rival-

Higher Bebington Mill in full working order

ry amongst the ladies who took in washing to get pieces of the old sails big enough to make large aprons to protect themselves when they were doing the washing. The mill property as we remember it contained large graneries, storage buildings for the mill waggons and stabling for the horses. In the Johnson's time, as well as the locally grown grain much, particularly the corn, was imported and was collected from the docks and the horse drawn waggons were well used bringing it to the mill. Both flour and meal (animal feeds) produced had to be delivered to customers by these waggons.

Even in such favourable positions as Higher Bebington, wind power could not always be relied on to provide power in the right amount, just when it is needed. In the 1880's Johnson invested in a Fowler 'Portable' steam engine, which became known as "Wirral Lassie" to drive the stones, when the wind was not right. The success of this was sufficient for him to go one step further and install a stationary steam-engine in the mill that could be called on in times of need.To generate the steam there was a boiler-house with a tall brick chimney that was about as high as the mill itself.The chimney stood until after WW2, though long disused. This meant that "Wirral Lassie" could be used for other purposes, so he invested in a threshing machine which, with "Wirral Lassie" he hired out to local farmers to help them, and provided additional revenue for the mill. It is intriguing that in a Directory at that time Johnson is described as "Corn Miller (Wind and Water)", the compiler must have been thinking of the traditional water-mills such as Bromborough and credited Higher Bebington with being similar, rather than STEAM driven The mill has seen merrymaking as well as the hard work.

When it was son Harry's 21st Birthday, Johnson decided to arrange a party for him and his friends and relations. The problem was, where? So, the mill buildings were brought into use. The granery and out buildings were cleared to give space for games, dancing and refreshments; additional lanterns were brought in and candles put in holders in the walls. The party started in the early evening and went on till near dawn the next day. By that time, the vibrations from the games and dancing had stirred up the flour dust from between the boards and out of all the nooks and crannies, so that all the guests went home grey-haired and the men's suits were all a uniform pale grey!

On Mill Brow, opposite the mill, was Mill House.This was designed and built by Alf Lee for the Johnsons just after they decided to close the mill. It was a very substantial house, with 8 bedrooms. It had, as was usual in houses of that era, a large 'living kitchen' with a cast iron range for heating and cooking, and plenty of space for a large family to sit round the table at meals. Over the front door was a timber porch on the lintel of which was carved,- "A.D. '09". This was taken by many people to mean that the house had been built in 1809, but in fact when Alf Lee was building the porch at Mr Johnson's request to make it look more like a 'private' residence with having stopped working the mill, he put this date on with the remark "Just to keep 'em guessing!", and it did.

Apart from 'Mill House' there were various cottages on the Eastern side of Mill Brow. Until just after Johnson took over the mill, many were in poor condition and frequently drew the attention of the Medical Officer of Health on his regular visits. Some of the tenants apparently paid no rent, had not done so for some considerable time and it was not clear who owned several of the cottages. In common with very many of the cottagers in the village, many of them kept pigs and these gave rise to criticism of the proximity of the styes to the cottages. At the Southern end were two cottages which "belong to the Overseersof the Poor", and three others "used by vagrants who turn up and take possession when they require them". In total, there were something like 20 cottages.

When Mill House was built, there was considerable tidying up and rebuilding of the cottage properties, fewer in number and of better standard. After the mill stopped working, the cap slowly disintegrated in the weather and storms, and in 1916 the sails were removed as they were becoming dangerous.The main difficulty in doing this was the hardness of the timbers; it is said that the men doing the job spent more time sharpening their saws than in sawing. Efforts were made in 1935/6 by the Bebington Ratepayers' Association to have the Mill preserved, but with the then preference for 'Tidying up' and 'Improving' this was of no avail, and then WW2 prevented further action until it was too late. During both WW1 and WW2 the tower was used as a lookout-post. The Williams brothers, Reg and Sam, used the out-buildings from when they acquired it in 1947 for storage and work-space of their building business until Reg Willams died in 1966, when Sam decided to sell the property. Reg Williams will be remembered for his service on the local Council; he was elected an Alderman and served as Mayor of Bebington in 1944/5. In April 1966 he became the fourth Freeman of Bebington in recognition of his long Public Services.

The mill and its associated property was Scheduled as being of special historical interest. Much of the machinery and equipment was still in the mill, but the mill itself was in very poor overall condition so, with the necessary statutary notice given it was demolished in March 1968. This was a very sad day in the village, not just amongst the older residents who had known it in better times, but also younger ones who saw it as a symbol of the community.

Humans were not the only ones to miss the mill; one lady who had lived all her life with the view of it from her living room window realised this from the first evening after it had gone, and for four or five weeks after that. She saw that just as dusk fell, the feral pigeons came over, circled two or three times as they always had done, and then with their feet down, 'in landing position', they frantically tried to land in their accustomed roosting places on the top of the non-existant mill.

5

School Lane

'The Tin Chapel' and Weston's Shop

Just beyond the four cottages that had formed the original "Windmill" inn, roughly in the corner of the present "George" carpark and facing up Village Road, was the "Tin Chapel" as it was called in the village. As the name suggests, it was built entirely of corrugated iron panels, except for its wooden porch. This was, until 1939, when the land was redeveloped for "The George", the local Methodist Church. It then moved to the old school at the Southern end of School Lane. A photograph of their last Harvest Festival in 1938 shows a wonderful display of fruit and vegetables that would delight the judges at any garden produce contest. The Chapel was used for other meetings; many of the 'Lads' recollect the Lantern Shows at 1p a time, and the jostling to get a good seat!

Adjacent to the Chapel, the first house in School Lane was Mr William Weston's general grocery shop. He also had a small-holding at the end of the lane. His Mother Harriet and his sister Dolly looked after the shop most of the time, and in later years he did his deliveries in a Morris van over quite a wide area. He would use the van to help transport the children to Arrowe Park on their Sunday School Outings. To liven up meals, children would be sent to get 'Two pennyworth of piccalilli and red cabbage' from the shop. Mr Weston would never see a family on hard times go without food. He closed the shop after 43 years in 1963 and it was demolished along with the other five cottages in that row.

Mr Weston was a mainstay of the Methodist Church in the village and visiting Ministers would be entertained at his house and use his parlour as the Vestry before going to the Chapel to take a service.

Mr Weston's Grocery Shop' School Lane

Earlier in its life the shop was owned by Mr Adam Telford. Mr Telford was renowned for his personal cleanliness and that of his shop, in spite of the fact that in addition to the grocery he had a coal-merchant's business on the piece of land between the shop and the Chapel. The front of this cottage, and hence the shop window, faced onto School Lane: all the other five in this row had their backs with a small yard, and outside 'privie', to Village Road. Their 'fronts' had neat, good sized gardens with open views over Wirral to Liverpool and down the Mersey to Runcorn.

The Small Cottages

Immediately beyond these was a row of very small cottages, the row being 'End-on' to the road. These were older, simple dwellings, known as Lightbound's Cottages as they had been 'tied' to the mill. One lady I talked to recalled her childhood in one of them at the end of the 19th century; her father was the Foreman in the quarries at the time. He finished work on a Saturday night at 6 pm, collected his week's money, came home, had his meal and was then off to the 'Local'. As soon as he had gone, Mother collected the children together ready for

Lightbound's cottages 'end-on' to school Lane, with some of the modern houses that were to replace them

Higher Bebington Harvest Festival Display 1938, the last one at the 'Tin Chapel'.

Higher Bebington Wesleyan Methodist Sunday School 1903

bed. There was only one upper room where the whole family slept, and access to this was by a ladder through a square hole in the living room ceiling, there were no 'stairs' as we know them. They all climbed up, and then Mother pulled up the ladder behind her, so that when Father returned from his night out he had to stay down below until he had slept it off!

More or less opposite these cottages was an abattoir; sheep and cattle would be 'walked' from Spital Station to the holding pens there. It was not at all unusual for the odd one to stray into the houses in School Lane if their doors were left open. Between Lightbound's cottages and Mill terrace were half a dozen small '2 up, 2 down' cottages that were demolished soon after WW2.

Mill Terrace and Tyson's Field

At the end of School Lane, on the left, is Mill Terrace. This property was built about 1896-1900 and must have been in sharp contrast to the older, smaller cottages around the mill area. The houses are well built in red brick, had good gardens, front and rear, and open views to

Eastham and beyond. One lady who lived there all her life from the time they were built, remembered when she was about 7 years old moving into it with her parents as soon as it was finished. The aspect from Mill Terrace has changed markedly in more recent years from being an open fieldscape. Boultons the builders had a materials store and offices there for a considerable time and then it was used by the Eastham Timber Company, before being developed as Shallmarsh Road. Originally this was Tyson's, or Gampy's Field. Gampy, from Gampy Tyson who was tall and had a long white beard, not unlike Abraham Lincoln. He lived in Village Road and kept chickens and pigs. It was on this field that all the outdoor events of the village, sports days, football matches such as those of the Higher Bebington 'Lilly Whites' in the 1920-30's, and so on took place.

Mrs Tyson had a cow and used to sell milk as she led it through the village, straight from the cow! Another part of her trade was to cut small blocks of the softer yellow stone that was not good enough for building work, from by the quarries to sell door to door for 'holy stoning' the front door-steps. She also had a string of donkeys grazing on the field; these she would take to Raby Mere or Eastham Ferry at weekends and holidays to hire for rides by the trippers who went there.

For Queen Victoria's Diamond Jubilee in 1897, they had a great bonfire here as part of the celebrations. It seemed a good idea then, to do the same thing to celebrate the Coronation of Edward VII on 2nd June 1902 in a similar way. Jack Lee, the village contractor,erected the pile that was to have been the bonfire on the field, right in front of Mill Terrace. This was an ill-fated venture. Photographs taken at the time show it to be over 40 feet high and about 25 feet across at the base with ladders fastened to it for the workmen to take more material up to the top. The main work was almost finished on that day and just before mid-day three men were hauling barrels of hot pitch to pour over it, when the whole structure collapsed. George Williams, who was 32, was trapped under a beam George Owen dragged him out, but he died in the ambulance that was taking him to hospital just as it passed his house. His widow, Hanna, gave birth to a daughter, Georgina, five weeks later. A memorial stone to him was erected in the Church yard by subscription from the people of the village. George Owen was later awarded the Humane Society Life-Saving Medal for his act of courage,

The ill-fated bonfire on Tyson's field, intended to celebrate King Edward VII's Coronation

this was presented by Mr W.H.Lever, of Lever Brothers. Mr Jim Appleton, Mr Connor and Mr Joynson were each injured. Because of the tragedy, the celebrations were cancelled. The material was burned off during the day and although it was well into the field, the heat was such that it blistered the paint on the houses in Mill Terrace.

The Old Schools

To many people in the village the schools on Mill Road are still 'The New Schools' even though they were built in 1913. The building at the end of School Lane on the Western side, although it has been the Methodist Chapel since before WW2, is refered to as 'The Old Schools', but in its day, better known as 'The College' or 'The Academy'.

Higher Bebington Church Schools, now the Methodist Meeting Rooms

The School was built in 1845. Major Orred,who lived at Lavant House in Chichester, but owned various lands in this area and regarded himself as in a Lord of the Manor position, gave the land for the School under the "School Sites" Act of 1841, which afforded special facilities for the transfer of land for school purposes by limited owners. The gift was made,

"Upon the condition that the Bible be read and the Scriptures taught

Group III of the Village School about 100 years ago

in the Schools, along with the Doctrines and Principles of the Church of England". The building cost £235, of whch £118 was raised by Public Subscription, the balance was provided by The Reverend Dr Thomas Fisher Redhead of St Peter's, Rock Ferry, which was then the Parish Church. As well as catering for the school, it was used for the local Sunday School, and for meetings of societies and committees. The school-master had a comfortable house just behind the school and this has been modified and extended over the years. A detailed history of the school has been written by F.P. Gopsil, so we will only make some passing notes here.

The first Inspection of the schools was in 1874 when the Diocesan Inspector reported to the Trustees, with a copy to the Bishop, on the Religious Knowledge of the pupils. Though he was well pleased with the Infants School he obviously did not find the, perhaps unreasonably, high standard he anticipated in the Mixed School. He conceded that the 'slate work' was "tolerably accurate", but of the eight pupils who wrote a subject on paper, "the best answers were rather disappointing".

However, amongst the two or three pupils singled out for mention was John Lee who, some forty years later was to particpate in the building of the New Schools on Mill Road.

Perhaps as a result of general experience on both sides the Inspector's reports became more encouraging as the years passed. Non-the-less, in the present day criticism of the infants for inaccurate and indistinct repetition of the Catechism seems a little hard. He does concede that they may be at a disadvantage in 'Having their Scripture Lesson at the end of afternoon School, when tired and restless'.

Within two or three years, the Reports became quite glowing, "Miss Baines deserving credit for the pains she has taken with the Infants", and praise for the knowledge of the Prayer Book Services in the Mixed School. It is interesting to note that until near the turn of the century, when the situation did improve somewhat, the average attendance was only between half and two-thirds of those on the books. At that time it was agreed that the school would take pauper children from the Workhouse, provided that The Union paid for them. In 1874 four of them attended.

In the 1870's there were several changes of teacher for the infants and this was seen as a reason for such short-comngs as were found,until in 1879 he reported that "The children were in capital order,-saying their Repetition Texts with commendable distinctnes and correctness". In that year, we see Henry B Johnson, the miller's son mentioned as worthy of commendation in the Infants' School. Two years later, Josiah Peers, who was to become the Village Smith, sing in the Church choir and later be their Policeman, being "mentioned honourably".

Staff shortages were a continuing problem, but the standard of the school received obvious praise from the Inspector; "The precision and method with which the School is worked is remarkable, and the Master deserves credit for what I believe to be much patient and conscientious work". It is perhaps a little surprising, with the general picture we tend to form of the schools in those days, to find the Inspector commenting that the children were not natural enough, not at their ease, "There is a stiffness of drill about their work, an unpleasant feature in the Infants". We should obviously be careful in making sweeping generalisations about education methods of the time.

By 1888 the Inspector reported that "This is one of the best Infants Schools I have ever examined, either in this or the Diocese of Durham and Newcastle", praise indeed. The naturalness and ease of the children obviously received attention and was commented on particularly in the 1901 Inspection, when they "Answered more naturally and freely than I ever remember previously". Singing must have been regarded as an important subject, for "The singing, as usual, was excellent and the Anthem 'I know that my Redeemer liveth' could not have been better executed by a first rate choir!".

With the implementation of the 1902 Education Act the new managing body of the School was constituted at its first meeting at Beechworth House at 8 pm on Thursday 24th September 1903.

The members of this body were;

The Revd L.W.Troughton (ex officio as Vicar of Parish)

Mr A.Mathews ⎫   Foundation
Mr R.R.Woodcock ⎬   Managers.
Mr T.Nickels ⎭

Mr J.J.Evans,   Appointed by County Council.
Mr J.V.Hodgson   Appointed by Urban District Council.

It was agreed that the Vicar be Chairman and Official Correspondent; Mr Thos. Nickels was appointed Treasurer.

Probably taking advantage of the the change over, Mr Troughton put forward the need for change in staff of the Mixed School. The Headmaster (Mr Jones) had told him that from the beginning of the school year the size of the Standards would make it impossible for the present staff to teach efficiently. He recommended that in place of Miss Berth Maclure, an assistant teacher, a male ex-pupil teacher should be obtained to wield more efficient discipline over the older boys. The County Authourity evidently did not support these views for no such changes were made. It would seem even then, it was difficult to pin down officials; Mr Troughton had had no reply from Mr Ward of Chester to correspondence about this and although he travelled there specifically to see Mr Ward, he "Could not find him"! However, Miss Maclure resigned a month later and Mrs Jones (the Headmaster's wife) was asked to be a temporary teacher at £50 p.a. until a permanent appointment could be made. As the year moved on, life became apparent in the County Offices, when they refused to foot the bill of £3 for

Attendance Prizes that were already promised and awarded by the school under arrangements that existed before the new Act. The School Managers in their turn snubbed the proposal from the County that Schools achieving certain attendance levels should give a half-holiday as an inducement to continued good performance. Whenever there are changes in responsibilities and loyalties at times such as these, financial matters tend to become somewhat involved. An Endowment had been made by the Lord of the Manor of Bebington some 200 years earlier for 'School Purposes'. Now that Higher Bebington had been a separate Parish for quite a number of years, though the subject of money was a delicate one, the Managers decided to look into it to see to what extent Higher Bebington School should be benefiting. After much involved correspondence, Mr Walter Peel of the Registrar's Office in Liverpool replied on behalf of Canon Fielden, Vicar of St Andrew's and one of the Trustees, to state that if the Managers of Bebington and New Ferry Schools were willing, £10 per annum could be paid to Higher Bebington. The sum was obviously not to be parted with very readily and in 1907 we see that the matter was still not settled. On the brighter side, by the end of 1903 the Director of Education wrote to the Managers asking that the Headmaster's salary be increased to £113 per annum, including rent and Superannuation Fee.

By now December had arrived, and Mr J.J.Gray having visited the school complained that the infants' room was too cold,- it was agreed that this should be looked into. At the time there was only a single fireplace in the room for about 85 infants, so it was agreed that Messrs Mawby of Birkenhead should install a "Fire grate stove" on the opposite side of the room at a cost of £6-10-0d.

The Government, as opposed to the Diocesan, Inspector's Report on the school for 1903 shows that in the Infants "Fair progress is being made", while in the Mixed School although instruction is still "Lacking in both vigor and intelligence in the Third Class, the work on the whole is very fairly satisfactory". He was not particularly satisfied with the general state of the building, however, "Both light and windows want thorough cleansing, the Boys 'Offices' need reconstruction and their cloakroom accommodation is insufficient". The County Authority looked into the whole problem of the condition of the school and the schoolmaster's house. As the year progressed, the work was put in hand, but the Inspector (Mr Howard) was still not satisfied when he was there in October 1904, so he wrote to the Managers again. At their November meeting they 'noted his letter' and agreed to take no further action on it!

The Clerk to the Guardians of the Workhouse (now Clatterbridge Hospital) wrote to the Managers in September 1904 saying that they intended sending 15 children from the Workhouse to the school. The Managers agreed to take them, subject to there being room in the rapidy filling school. Attendance averaged 140, another 18 double desks were ordered, and the Inspector directed that an additional Assistant Teacher be appointed to cope with the increase in the Mixed School, a Miss Williams from Llandudno was appointed.

The increase in the Headmaster's salary the previous year was to be eroded, the rent on his house was increased from £5 to £10 per annum; obviously costs, probably the repairs required by the County Sub-committee, were rising. Early in 1905 considerable further repairs and improvements to the school were recommended by the Inspector and the County, and the Managers were given 3 years to get these done. The yard was re-asphalted at a cost of £21, the ventilation improved and plain glass put in the windows of the Infants' room inplace of the coloured. In readiness for the winter, a new gas lamp bracket was fitted. All this was done within 12 months. In May 1905 the epidemic of measles was such that 50 children were absent; and the Medical Officer closed the school.

There were staffing problems that year, as those applicants for positions who were suitable tended to feel that the village was too remote. The problems from the difficulty in recruiting staff, of an ageing building and overcrowding were becoming acute, total attendance was now 263 pupils, well above the number that could be accommodated comfortably. This was emphasised in the Inspector of Schools Report of that year. In spite of this, he classed the School's performance as above average in the Authority's area. Quarry working was getting even closer to the property, and there was considerable hustle and bustle from the waggons right in front of the school taking the stone away. There were even suggestions that the quarry owners would seek the land on which the schoolmaster's house was built to extend their workings.

By March 1910 the Inspector (Mr J.H.Brown) reported that "The schools are inconveniently full. The population is growing and more accommodation is needed. Moreover, the situation of the school has become an undesirable one, owing to the noise and smoke from the crane engines of the quarry." All the previous critcisms were becoming more acute. In the light of this very lengthy and detailed critical report, it seems ironic that at the same meeting the Chairman reported that he had ordered a new bell! The Managers replied in a letter that they "found it impossible to carry out any of the improvements suggested seeing that the site is inadequate." This was the beginning of the end for the Old School, and in 1913 it was moved to its new premises in Mill Road.It was not until 1897 that School Lane was 'Adopted' by the local authority, prior to this it was little more than an access way for the mill and quarry properties, then on to Prospect Hill houses and through to Bracken Lane.

6

Prospect Hill

If we had continued from the end of School Lane along the track on the Eastern side of the quarries, we would have met the path that came across from Mount Road, and here was Prospect Hill. It was a community of about 15 houses that had been the homes of quarry workers and their families for many generations. In an 1874 report it was described as "13 cottages and two better class houses", one of these latter houses was probably that in which Mrs Oxton had set up her Inn some 30 years earlier. It is likely that the first settlement of quarrymen was in this area. It was known variously locally as "Bunkers' Hill", "The Common", or "The Old White City". From here the track went on to Bracken Lane, before Derwent Road was built. It was a place without luxuries, up to the late 1930's there was no gas or elecricity, cooking was done on the black-leaded grate or on primus type stoves, candles and oil-lamps gave the only light after dark. When electricity was installed just before WW2, it came via overhead cables with wires run down the walls from under the eaves. Each Whitsuntide all the cottages would be whitewashed, giving a bright outlook for the summer.

Most of the people who lived here were true "Fir-Bobs". Several of the men played in the village's football team, "The Lily Whites". Some residents remember as children, playing 'Houses and Shops', and using pieces of broken pottery as pretend money, white bits for pennies, and the blue and white for shillings. There was Mrs Furphy who was 'good' at sewing things' and could take an old coat to make a pair of boy's trousers for a shilling. Some of the cottages were pulled down in the late 1950's, the rest survived until 1979/80 when there was redevelopement of the area.

The 'White City' Cottages on Prospect Hill

The Quarries

Stone has been taken from this Eastern ridge of Wirral since Roman times, for decorative and memorial stones and for building. An inscribed slab from the tomb of a Centurian in the Grosvenor Museum in Chester is believed to have been taken from this area, and the Saxon cross at Neston is of this stone. Nearer home, of course, St Andrew's Church is a fine example from its original building and through the many additions and modifications over the centuries.

The coming of the Industrial Revolution brought greater demands for building stone of high quality, and this provided the incentive for the Stanleys to revitalise their quarries on the Storeton side of the ridge.The stone on the Storeton side was easier to extract in that this could be done by simply cutting into the hill-side and hauling out, rather than having to dig deeply into the ground. Their output was sufficient by the early 1830's that they had to consider the problems of transportation to more distant customers. It was this which led to them installing the tramway from those workings to a creek on the river Mersey from where the stone could be shipped to a wide area in the Northwest. A full account of this venture is given in Mr R.C.Jermy's book "The Storeton Tramway".

It was while a cutting was being made to take this line through the rock of the then disused small quarry just above Bracken Lane that the now renowned 'Footprint Bed' was found. These were formed by an animal which has been named 'Cheirotherium', meaning 'hand-footed' as the imprints look remarkably like those of hands, with a thumb sticking out. These prints were formed when the animals had walked on muddy ground, probably silt that overlaid the earlier deposited sands. Later, wind-blown sand covered these and over the eons became the beds of stone. The result was that CASTS of these animals' footprints were formed on the underside of the overlying rock, and it is these which were found. On these slabs can also be seen the marks where the animals' tails trailed, and the ripples that had formed on the silt on which they walked, just as we see ripples on the sands when we are on the beach and even the marks of rain drops. Footprints of at least ten different, smaller animals can be found on these beds, though these are not so easily seen or identified as those of the Cheirotherium.This

The 'Footprint' specimen, nearly 10 feet square, ready for sending to the British Museum in 1906

bed is about 80 feet below the surface, and stetches over a very wide area; in fact, prints which are almost certainly from the same animal have been exposed by natural erosion of the rocks on Hilbre Island only a few years ago. It is strange that no fossil remains of any such animal are known to have been found. Very many specimens have been taken over the years. There are examples in the Williamson Art Gallery, Liverpool Museum, The British Museum, Victoria Hall, Christ Church porch, and Mill Road Schools to name but a few.

It is common practice, when speaking of any of the workings on the ridge, singly or collectively, to group them all together and refer to them simply as the Storeton quarries. As we are concerned here with Higher Bebington let's make the correct differentiation between the different parts. All the workings on the West side of the road were the Storeton quarries, owned by the Stanleys and later the Brocklebanks.These ceased operation except for trivial amounts, around 1920. It was into this area that the waste from the first Mersey road tunnel was tipped, effectively 'killing two birds with one stone', if you will forgive the pun, by getting rid of about a million cubic yards of rubble, and restoring the quarry area to something like its former aspect at one fell swoop.

The Parish/administrative boundary runs along the Mount Road, thus the workings on the Eastern side are the Higher Bebington quarries. From where Mill Road joins Mount Road, along the Western edge of the Heather Bank property, was a small delph in which stone was worked, but this had ceased by the latter part of 19th century when Heather Bank House was built. At the Southern end of the ridge, where Broomleigh Close now stands in a delph, there had been the quarry through which the Stanley's tramway ran, so this must have been more or less worked-out by 1840, and is marked as 'Disused' on 1890's maps with a couple of cottages built in it. There were several cases of diphtheria at one of these cottages in the early 1900's and it was condemned to be demolished. The family who lived there payed 11/- a year rent. However, it still stands there today, much improved.

Prior to the present houses being built there had been a nursery garden there for some time.The Higher Bebington quarries of importance were those which operated between the Southern boundary of the abat-

71

toir property, now Millfield Close, and the footpath from Mount Road to Prospect Hill on the Northern edge of Broomleigh Close. The Eastern limit of the quarry was the path that continued from the end of School Lane, to give access to Prospect Hill houses and then on to what is now, Derwent Road. The main access to the quarries was just beyond the old Schools. In all they covered 5.5 acres.

The stone from all these quarries is a "Free-stone", this means that it has no natural cleavage planes, and so has the same strength in all directions. This is of great advantage in structural work, as it does not have to be laid in any particular orientation to avoid cracking under load.Dependent on the particular beds that were being worked, the colour of the stone ranged from the yellow, soft stone near the surface, to the good silvery white bed and then to the darker brown, lower bed. Within each bed, the colour was quite consistent. Of these, the yellow was the softer, weaker stone and not suitable for building work; some of it was used in lower quality walling, but most was broken up for aggregate. From this colouring the Higher Bebington quarries have been known at various times as "The Brown Stone Quarries", and "The Brown and White Stone Quarries".

The disadvantage of Free-stone is that with having no natural cleavage planes it cannot be 'split' out of its beds as some other stones can like, in an extreme example, slate. It has to be cut by some means; the use of explosives is limited by their shattering effects which not only wastes stone but could weaken the blocks produced.

There had been large scale operation in the Higher Bebington quarries for some considerable time, the stone was hand-cut from the beds and such cranes as there were being hand operated. But there was extensive scope for further working and improvements in operations.In 1905 the then owner, Mr Bullock, sold them to Mr Wells who had quarries in Liverpool that had been worked for some years, and he saw this as a worthwhile expansion of his interests. Mr Wells' Liverpool quarries had also originally been worked by hand, but soon after Liverpool started taking its water supply from Lake Vyrnwy and not from the bore holes within the city the water table rose markedly and made the quarries very wet to work. To improve the conditions Mr Wells imported steam driven stone cutting machines to minimise the amount of hand working necessary in the initial removal of stone from the beds. The machine was "The Wardwell Patent Channelling Machine" made in America. It had been widely used in both marble and sandstone quarries in the USA and proved its worth. They were ideal for working the sandstone in Mr Well's quarries.

George Wardwell worked for some 20 years for the "Steam Stone Cutter Company" in Rutland, Vermont and had several Patents on stone working machinery. This particular machine,ignoring its chimney, was only about 5 feet high, weighed a ton, and worked on a set of rails looking, at first impression, like a small railway locomotive.

There were reciprocating devices on both sides of it, in either or both of which could be clamped chisel ended cutters up to 14 feet long, which cut 'channels' about 4" wide in the rock, as it moved slowly by a geared drive along the rails. At the end of each run, the cutters were set deeper, the engine put into reverse, to deepen the channel on the return run. This was repeated until the desired depth of cut was reached. Any width of block could be cut by moving the rails the appropriate amount. There was the added advantage that the stone face as cut by the machine needed minimal dressing to make it suitable for architectural use. Stone wastage was small; only that from the narrow channel being lost and that could be sold as sand or aggregate.

This engine, needing three men to operate it, delivered 6 HP, using 4 cwt of coal each day. In one day it could cut a face up to 25 feet long and 14 feet deep; this is about 15-16 times as much as could be done without the machine. The use of these machines was regarded as sufficiently innovative that photographs of them in use at Higher Bebington were used in text books on quarrying at that time. However, the captioning of the picture in one book adds further to the confusion that (still) exists between Higher Bebington and Storeton quarries. Evidently the author had been in contact with Mr Wells at his home address in Bootle, and the caption reads, "Channelling machines working in Storeton quarry, Bootle, near Liverpool".

These machines were of sufficient interest to Industrial Archeologists that approaches were made to Mr Wells by a member of the local Museums Staff and the author suggesting that one should be preserved. However, as noted earlier, such was Mr Wells confidence that work would start again at the quarries "one day" that he took no action and the machines were simply scrapped when he died and the

A Channelling machine working the East-end of the quarry about 1905. This photograph was originally captioned 'Storeton Quarry, Bootle near Liverpool'

The Wardwell Channeller

property was sold. As soon as he started working the Higher Bebington quarries, Mr Wells brought one of these machines over to try it on this type of stone. Finding that it worked well, he ordered two more machines specifically for Higher Bebington. He also brought over the steam driven travelling crane which continued to operate for almost another 40 years at the North end of the quarry by the school. A new travelling crane with tracks running the length of the quarry on the East side was installed to facilitate moving of the stone in the cutting and storage area, and its subsequent loading for transport to customers. To raise the very large blocks of stone that could be so readily cut by these new machines, a massive fixed crane was installed near the centre of the quarry and this remained a landmark until the machinery was finally removed for scrap in 1971.

These stone cutting machines were not universally well received. Their regular chomp-chomp- chomp throughout the day became quite irritating to both pupils and teachers particularly in later years when the cutting face was nearer the North end of the quarry by the school. The culmination was when explosive charges were used to separate the blocks from the rock bed and more often than not all the ink-wells would jump out of their holes in the pupils' desks.

Many of those who worked at the quarry in its later years are remembered; Jacky Williams Foreman/cranedriver,and it was the whistle on his crane which he sounded as the "Hooter" for starting work at 8 am; Mr Preston who had the big crane under heavy load when a high wind caught it and it blew over. George Green would lower men in a skip to the workings at the bottom. Sammy Duckers and Edward Darlington who were rivers, that is, worked on splitting the blocks of stone that had been cut, to the sizes the customer wanted. Scotty Oswald was the Blacksmith; before working at the quarry he had worked with Jos Peers at the village smithy. He had to keep all the cutters in tip-top condition and be prepared to do any repairs necessary on the machinery. With having a good hot hearth, he made up the tea-cans; but on one occasion when he was putting them onto a scoop to be lowered into the quarry it swung unexpectedly and he overbalanced, fell into the workings and was killed. Jimmy Doyle operated the stone crusher that converted the scrap and small stone into coarse sand that could be sold to builders for aggregate.

*High winds and a heavy load caused the disastrous
collapse of the main central crane.*

Mr Wells, and after he died, his son Frank, came every day from Bootle. Mr Frank Wells was a retired major, and fully looked the part, always dressed 'The Gentleman'. The quarry was in production until 1940, when reduced demand and shortage of labour, both resulting from WW2, necessitated what Mr Wells anticpated at the time was to be a temporary closure. Even though work had finished, Mr Wells drove himself over at least twice a week, checked that all was in order, collected rents from some properties he had in the village, and often did little jobs for people, until he was in his 80's. He kept his machinery well protected with grease, to the extent that after 20 years or more it could have been put back into use with very little servicing. He kept the telephone line to "Wells F, White Freestone Quarry, Bebington, 608 2476" until he died in 1970. As late as the 1960's he had an enquiry from the PCC of a Wirral Church as to whether he could supply stone for them to build an additional aisle to their church. They did this because the church had been built of local stone, but very many years before. Mr Wells told them that the quarry was no longer in production, but he felt sure that there would be sufficient stone already cut, simply stacked in the holding area, that they could have this for the taking if it suited their purpose. As far as we know, he had no further communica-

BROWN AND WHITE STONE QUARRIES, HIGHER BEBINGTON, CHESHIRE.
CHARLES WELLS, PROPRIETOR.

The travelling crane in the Stock-yard

tion from them. It seems a shame that his offer was not taken up.

By the time work stopped the faces had moved well up to the Northern end and depths of 80- 100 feet had been reached. The stone was becoming less accessible and to have continued on an economic basis there would have had to have been major reorganisation of the service parts of the quarries to provide access to workable stone.On occasions, when cutting had been very close and deep adjacent to Mount Road there would be a collapse of the boundary wall and some of the road.

Apart from the necessary storage areas and sites for the cranes, the main service facillity was the smithy. This was a substantial building on the Eastern side, with two large hearths. There were anvils and all the necessary black-smith's tools, including a very big, hand operated drilling machine capable of making holes of large size in iron-work that would be required in maintaining the machinery at the quarry. This need was evident when one could see, for example, where new teeth had been made and bolted in on the gear wheels of the cranes to replace broken ones. The ₒood sized grindstone there was not, however, of local stone as this is too soft for effective grinding.

None of the good stone was wasted, only the unusable softest yellow stone from near the surface was put on the spoil heaps in the worked-out part of the quarry. Even some of this, together with the waste from cutting and shaping, was fed into the stone-crusher.The small stone and chippings, from cutting out the stone, to feed this was shovelled into large scoops, about four feet square and 18" deep to be hauled out of the quarry and emptied into its hopper. This was a mighty machine that stood high on large stone blocks between the loading area and the quarry itself. It was driven by a steam engine made by T. Robinson of Rochdale that Mr Wells had bought from Mr Henry Williams when he was upgrading his equipment at the Steam-mill in 1908; it continued in service in the quarry until 1940.

Stone from the quarry has been widely used in the construction of public buildings and private houses. Some of these of note are: Christ Church, Higher Bebington; St Hilary's, Wallasey; Southport GPO; Martin's Bank, Bootle; Westminster Bank, Birkdale; Martin's Bank, Birkdale; and Blundell Sands Hotel. Within the local area we have only to look at the many stone built houses, and the fine stone walls. The construction of walls such as we see round us is becoming all but a lost art.

As the quarries became neglected, brambles grew on the slopes of the waste heaps to give good pickings for the local lads in the autumn, you could get a basket full in about 10 minutes. The lower workings gradually filled with water, collected rubbish thrown in by passers-by, and nature slowly took over again. The local boys soon discovered that newts, frogs and small fish had settled in the waters at the bottom of the quarry, it was said that kingfishers nested in crevices in the rock faces, though I never saw one myself. What I did see was the ingenious method the lads used to catch the fish, newts and frogs from the pools. From the accumulated rubbish they would find a barrel or small oil drum and roll it into the water, and haul it out about half full. Then, by using old saucepans and similar containers that lay around, they scooped out the water, inspecting each pan-full carefully for any signs of life. Objects of interest were put into one of their jamjars, and the process repeated until the barrel had been emptied. Often there would be a rich "crop" of water creatures in the bottom part of the barrel, which would send up shouts of joy. They did all this of their own initiative, and learnt a lot; today we have formal 'Pond-dipping' outings doing more or less the same thing but we have to use proper nets and specimen bottles, not quite the same spirit of adventure.

At about the same time that the 'Lads' did this, the edge of the 'Foot-print' bed was exposed a few feet above the water at the bottom of the quarry. Much of the marl (old silt on which the animals had walked) had washed away from between the beds, leaving a gap of some 2 feet. If you hung on very carefully over the edge of the adjacent rock, you could look on the underside of the upper rock and see the foot-casts. Though they are now under a lot of infill, they are still there; I wonder whether anyone will ever get down that far again to see them? After Mr Frank Wells died the property was sold, complete infilling effected, has passed through various hands and been the object of all sorts of tests to check the levels of methane emanating from the decomposition of the vegetable matter that is buried deep in the depths of the quarry. At present a permeable covering is being laid over the surface so that any gases formed can escape safely whilst allowing rainwater to sink in. The whole area can then be used as an 'open

The flooded East-end of the quarries after they had ceased operation. The 'Footprint-bed' a few feet above the water.

space', until it can be pronounced suitable land for development. There are not likely to be any Ghosts around there, or are there? What about those animals that roamed some 80 feet under the garden, a few million years ago?

7

'Storeton Road' The Top Part of Village Road

From its junction with Mill Road, to its Westerly end, what is now a continuation of (The) Village Road, was originally called Storeton, or Stourton, Road or Lane.

The 'Tiny Inn' and Griffiths' Dairy.

On the Western corner of School Lane with Village Road is now a private house. It was almost entirely rebuilt a few years ago in this form, losing its 'shop' windows and door on the corner. However, many will remember it as Griffiths's Dairy which was there until 1964, when Mr Griffiths retired and closed the shop. But let us look a little further back in its history, at the changes that have taken place. In the early 1870's it was a Beer house called "The Tiny Inn". The Licensing Returns of the time refer to it being in Storeton Road, the name given to the upper part of Village Road, as it was the route to Storeton which has long had associations with Higher Bebington. The License was for the sale of Beer, Ale and Porter only, no wines or spirits, but included 'Off-Sales'. In 1891 it was a 'Free house' owned by Catherine Williams of Chester Road, Leighton, with Samuel Peers as Licencee. Although it had one stable and one stall, it did not provide any bed or accommodation for travellers. Samuel Peers was the father of Josiah Peers, the village smith of King's Brow. As a sideline, Samuel did some cobbling and it was the presence of his pot of cobblers wax kept melted ready for use on the hearth that gave the Inn its nick-name in the village of "The Wax Pot". This must have been a family leaning as his brother William Peers in Storeton was a shoe-maker, not just a repairer, he made boots for the Policemen. One of the most prized possessions was to have a pair of William Peers' boots, they were called 'a pair of Billy Peers'. However, some patrons of the Inn claimed it had yet another name, 'The Glue Pot', because it got so crowded in such a small house that once you got in, particularly on a Saturday night, you were 'stuck' there!

In August 1897 Yates Castle Brewery, (John Smith's Tadcaster Brewery Ltd) bought the property. They fixed a large sign-board the full length of the Village Road side of the house to the eaves carrying the name "TINY INN", above the words "YATES TADCASTRER ALES". The licence was transfered to William Witard but he only held it for a short time as on 18th May 1900 we hear that William Cox was the licencee and was convicted of allowing drunken behaviour on the premises. William James Townson followed him.

Thomas Williams Bakery and Grocery Store in Village Road, with Griffiths' Dairy (the Tiny Inn) to the left, on the corner of School Lane

A fine Milk Bowl at Griffiths' Dairy

At the beginning of the century Mr Saxby is remembered as the licencee. One Saturday night he went to bed as usual and put his gold watch under his pillow. However, in the early hours a thief broke in and stole the watch. Although this did not disturb Mr Saxby, the movements disturbed Sweep, the dog at the bakery next door, who barked and woke Mr Saxby. But the thief had planned to delay anyone chasing him by putting a couple of chairs on the stairs behind him, and got clean away with it. This was seen as particularly brazen, as the Village Policeman only lived across the road in the middle house of Aigburth View

While Yates Brewery were the owners, the facilities were improved. By 1903 not only was there an additional stall in the yard, but beds for two travellers were available and 'Refreshments for six persons' was provided.The Inn played a full part in the social life of the village. It was here that the football teams changed on Saturday afternoons before going along to Tyson's Field for the match. As if to round off the day, in spite of its small size, there were Saturday night 'Hops', they could hardly be called dances, in the back room of the Inn. Admission was 6d, and the music was provided by a banjo. The last licencee was Kitty (Sugar) Williams, until the Inn closed early in 1911. In its later years it was suspected by the Authorities of being the meeting place of poachers and vagrants, and this probably led to its closure.Its subsequent change of use must surely be unique in the history of the Licencing trade. It became a Dairy, even though the property was still owned for another 40 odd years by the Brewery.

Griffiths's Dairy came from very small beginings. A Mrs Henshaw, who was blind and had been left a young widow with a large family kept a cow in a delph, long since filled in and modern houses built on it, on Mount Road. A son helped her with the milking and general work and she sold the milk. Most of her customers she knew by the sound of their voices, but anyone, particlarly the young children who were usually sent for the milk, she recognised instantly by the feel of their face. A daughter of Mrs Henshaw married Charles (Charlie) Griffiths, and they helped the trade develop. By the time their son Jack Griffiths took it over it was the flourishing business that we all remember being carried on from what had been 'The Tiny Inn', with the very lovely decorated milk-bowl that stood in the window. For the greater time this was a dairy, the milk was delivered in the large pails, and the measuring laddles used to put it into the customers jugs. Later they moved to one of the modern shops on King's Road. After Mr Jack Griffiths died, his widow changed the shop to a Florists, and fittingly called it *Fir-Bobs* .

Bill Head from Henry Williams' mill

William's Bakery and Steam mill.

Immediately above the"Tiny Inn"/Griffiths' Dairy is a large, three storey building with a commodious waggon entrance through it. This was built about 1860 for Thomas Williams to be his bakery and gro-cery shop. His flour came from the village mill and others further afield. Work here was hard: in November 1875, his Journeyman Baker, "a hale healthy man 26 years old was lifting a sack of flour,weighing probably 180 lbs from the cart in front of his Master's shop, he got it on his back and nearly into the shop when he staggered and fell, became blue in the face and died in about ten minutes.".

Looking towards the top of Village Road; Williams' Terrace on the left, Henry Williams' steam mill on the right and the Police notice Board in front of their house on Aigburth View in front of it.

Business was successful, and in the 1880's Williams decided that he would be better producing his own flours, and selling any surplus to other bakers. So he had a steam-driven mill erected on the other side of the road, immediately above where house No 54 now stands, on the East side of what was then Youd's Yard, a court of several cottages, various barns and pig-styes. This involved the removal of the small Chapel that stood there and erection of the 'Tin Chapel' we have mentioned, next to Weston's shop on the end of School Lane to take its place.

The mill extended well back from the road, and included a spacious granary that went as far as the footpath which goes from Mill Road corner along the ends of the gardens of the cottages on the North side of Village Road. Apart from the usual hoist on the road end of the mill for delivery of grains and shipment of flour and meal, there was access to the mill via the path into the Court, which was then recobbled and large paving slabs put on the lines where the waggon wheels would run, to take their heavy wear; until No 58 was demolished in 1998, this path could still be seen and one of the old mill stones was buried in it. On the Bill-heads Henry used there was an illustration of the mill which showed an access-way on the Eastern side as well.Backing onto this access way to the mill, where there is the garden of No 54, was erected a terrace of three houses called Aigurth View. In the late 19th C and early 20th C the middle one of these was the County Constabulary Station, with its large notice board by the front of the mill. On the land in front of these houses prior to 1948, overlooking Mill Road/Village Road corner, stood the British Legion Club.

Thomas Williams and his wife had a daughter, Mary, and four sons; Henry, William, Thomas and Edward. When these were young they had two girls as domestc servants, and a boy of 14 from the Workhouse training to be a baker. As the children grew older they helped in the house and business. William played a major part in this. The Williams' bakery became renouned throughout Wirral, and many 'Boys' in the village to whom I have spoken can remember helping with deliveries from the horse drawn van after school to Storeton, Brimstage and sometimes as far as Heswall or Willaston, to earn pocket money. Thomas' son William, who lived at 'Glent Villas' higher up the road, joined him in the business and it eventually passed to him. He was rather deaf and known, rather disrespectfully, as 'Baldy Billy' by the Boys of the village. His appearance was always very smart, with his blue and white striped apron, well starched cuffs and straw hat.His baker and roundsman was Johny Smith. The shop included a grocery; the 'boys' of the village would tell tales about William's deafness, such as being sent by their mother for a quarter of tea. Williams would ask in his loud voice:

"Yes, what do you want?"

"A quarter of tea, please",

"Speak up, Boy, what do you want?",

The request was repeated very loudly and distinctly "My mother wants a quarter of tea",

"Yes, does she want it sliced thick or thin?"

Pork pies were a speciality, and black puddings, of course. These were made on Thursdays for sale on Fridays, not just to provide for the weekend, but mainly because there was little money to spare in the middle of the week. Villagers would take their own bread dough to be baked, at a penny a loaf. A tag was put in the edge of each tin to identify whose loaves they were. At Christmas time the ovens would cope with their customers' Christmas cakes as well as their bread. Just before 1900, Henry took over full control of the steam mills, and in 1904 he married. His flour mills and his flour were widely advertised:

Williams Wirral Wheaten Flour,

Milled From the Choicest Selected English Wheats,

Grown In The Wirral Peninsula,

Now Being Supplied to The Leading Cafes in Liverpool

Henry had teams of horses for his lorries, and on holidays such as Whitsuntide, these were elaborately groomed and decorated as floats to take the village children on their Treats. He was also an innovator; he pioneered the use of steam lorries in the area. It was only a few years ago that his Grandson found a photograph of one of these, taken by the Birkenhead photographer Mr R.Morris outside his studios in Conway Street, just after Henry had taken delivery of it. Grain and flour was also stored in the large out-buildings behind the house on the other side of the road, that had been built for Mr Lewis, and became the Post Office. For a time Henry had Mill Butt Farm, and reared large numbers of pigs there. He sold grain to one of the then Vicar's brothers who kept a poultry business on the land behind the Vicarage. Unfortunately, Henry died in 1914 having been married only 10 years earlier, and the mill closed down.The mill could not be sold as a 'going concern', so the machinery was sold. The building was only used for storage until it was demolished in 1929. The list of items for sale makes interesting reading :(see facing page)

In the 1920's the whole building of the bakery and the grocery shop was taken over by the Cooperative Society and they remained there until their new shop on the corner of Town Lane was opened in the late 1950's.The premises have served several ventures since then, a commercial photographers, Alun Macdonalds the builders, and is now used by Storeton Developements. Immediately above the shop, where is now the business car-park, there was a row of eight terrace houses end-on to the road, facing West. This was Williams' Terrace,or Williams' Entry as it was also known, but locally called 'Aunt's Row' as it was built/owned by an Aunt of the Williams. Less respectfully, it was often

List of Milling Machinery For
Sale
And on View atThe Corn Mills
Higher Bebington

Boiler. 24 x 6ft., 3ft flue. No 1 Cornish, built in 1902 for the present position by the Oldham Boiler Works Co. Tested to 220 lbs., with a working press.,of 120 lbs., per sq in. Insured by the National Boiler and General Insurance Co. Manchester. The boiler is complete with all fittings and mountings. Last report from Boiler Inspector was absolutely faultless. Report can be seen. Also firebrick bed, flues and brick boiler cover if required.

Small Boiler.   Used as water tank.

Engine. Single cylinder, about 60 H.P. with Griffith feed heater, made by Fawcett & Co., Preston.

Worthington Pump.

Crab engine. 4½ H.P.

Disintegrator. 2½. Made by Christy & Morris, bought by owner in 1906. Ten sacks per hour, complete with hoppers etc., as per working order.

Meal Sifter and Elevators. with hoppers etc.

Stone Corn Crusher. by Anthony Stevenson, Cheshire. 4 ft dia. in ironframes, with shafting and bevelled gear wheels. Also additional pair of mill stones 4 ft. diameter.

Friction Hoist. to lift 5 cwt.

Crab Winch. to lift 3 cwt.

Hay Cutter. 3 blades, by Richmond & Chandler, with Climax Patent safety feeder Shafting. about 60 ft. 2½" dia. brackets & couplings.

All *Machines, complete with counter shafts & belts.*

One of Henry Williams' steam lorries

referred to as 'Cabbage Row'. In the house at the road end in the 1880's, before the Constabulary Station was set up in Aigburth View, the village Policeman Mr Woodroffe lived. These houses were all pulled down in 1963. On the Western side of Youd's Yard was a cottage, No 58 Village road, which was demolished in 1998, that in the 1870's had been Peter Whitehead's shop, and he also ran it as a Beer House.

Now let's digress a little. At that time in New Ferry, John and Ann Edge had a butcher's shop, that had been established in the 1850's. The Edge family are still running the same business, today. Some of their stock was brought from Delamere by a John Whieldon and his brother, to be slaughtered there. When they brought the stock over, the Whieldons would stay a while dressing and preparing the carcases. Later, in the mid-1870's John set up his own butcher's shop at 85 Old Chester Road in Tranmere. Business prospered, a second shop was opened in Tranmere at 174 Peel Street, and by the turn of the century a third, run by John Whieldon Jnr., at 22 Union Street. John Snr., spread his interests still further v.ith a shop in Heswall, and from that by 1902 had set up at No 58 Storeton (Village) Road in Higher Bebington. He made this a centre, building a slaughter house at the far end of the garden that remained more or less as when he used it with its hanging rail and large hooks and a heavy winch for hauling the carcases,until the cottage was demolished in 1998. This was the beginning of Whieldon's The Butcher's in Higher Bebington.

The Post Office

Mention has already been made of a Post Office at various times, and as it is evident that it was in different places over the years, it is perhaps best to look at its history overall. Through enemy action in WW2 a large part of the Post Office records in Liverpool were destroyed; however, through the help of local residents and families of previous Postmasters, a fair idea of its history in Higher Bebington has been pieced together.

White's Directory for 1851 says that the Post Office is "at Mr Dakin's in King Street, Rock Ferry", that is, quite likely in the same place as the present Rock Ferry Post Office. This was when what is

No. 58 Village Road, where John Wheldon started his Butcher's business in the village in the early 1900's.

Mr J Shaw's Provision shop that included the first Post Office.

Miss Sumnall at the front of her mother's Grocery shop/ Post Office on Tee Hey Lane in the early 1930's.

now Rock Ferry was part of Higher Bebington under the Birkenhead organisation of districts. It remained there until the local boundaries were reorganised in 1877 and the Bebington Ward of Birkenhead was ceded to the Urban District Council of Higher Bebington.

The first Post Office in the village was established about 1880 at Mr Joseph Shaw's, now No 79 Village Road. He had this quite large property built some years earlier as his house and shop. He was not only a Provision Dealer, but also an Agent for the Prudential Assurance Co. His wife managed the shop and when they took on the Post Office, his daughter became the Post Mistress. Much good natured banter was made of the name of the next Post Master, he was Adam Swindell!

As built, the Post Office had a large central front door. Some time after the house ceased to be the office, this was bricked up and a wall type Post-box put in there.This was moved to the garden wall of the house in the 1960's and then, when this was developed for new houses it was transfered to the Village Road end of Mill Road.

In 1907 Mrs Joynson took on the office and in 1910 it was moved to No 45 Village Road, opposite Mercer's cottage. Soon after this a Telephone was installed; the large sign-board of "The Bell Telephone Company" can be seen over the door on photographs taken about this time. Mrs Joynson and her husband moved to Mill Butt Farm at the beginning of WW1, and then Mrs Peers, wife of the village smith became Post Mistress. She, like Mrs Joynson, had left school when she was 11.

Both Mrs Joynson and Mrs Peers, and later Miss Jenny Peers who took over the office from her mother, performed considerable service for the Irish labourers who worked in the area. Many of them could neither read nor write, so it often fell to the Postmistress to read their letters to them, and she would then take down at dictation the replies to their families in Ireland. In 1912/13 the Office returned to its original location at No 79 Village Road, where it remained until it moved in the 1920's to a cottage that stood adjacent to the site of the present Post Office, on Tee Hey Lane, which was Mrs Sumnall's general shop and she became Post Mistress. A photograph taken in 1931 shows four of the then popular enamelled signs on the wall, these read;

> Post Office For Money Orders, Savings Bank, Parcel Post and Insurance and Annuity Business

> Post Office B.A Sumnall, Licensed to sell stamps.

> Public Telephone

> Support Brooke Bond's efforts to bring down Tea prices

The present office was built in 1932 when the row of shops replaced the old cottages.A point that might well be made here is on the danger of using maps as evidence for dating changes. Even though the Post Office had not been at No 79 Village Road for some 50 years, one particular publisher's local street map dated 1970 still showed it there!

The Traveller's Rest

The Travellers' Rest is an Inn that, at least outwardly, has remained unchanged over the years. Its beginnings are not known, but from its position and its name it could well be, in fact, a travellers' resting place on the ridge road from Birkenhead across to central Wirral, although until it was taken over by The Birkenhead Brewery it had no accommodation for travellers other than its beer. It was definitely there in 1860, the licensee is recorded as being James Ecclestone. The property was purchased by The Birkenhead Brewery Co Ltd in 1877, and the adjoining cottage absorbed into the premises in 1893 when John Hamer held the licence.By 1905 a stable and three stalls were available and it was a "good house accommodation for supplying refreshments"

That it did act as a 'Rest' has been confirmed by several residents who lived further along the road, particularly on Saturday nights after a night-out at 'The Argyle' in Birkenhead, when people would pull-up in their pony and trap for their own refreshment while giving the pony time to get its breath back after the long pull up Borough Road and Mount Road. It was fair game for the boys of the village to hang about and offer to hold the horse's head, for a suitable reward, whilst the owner went into the Inn. On one occasion, one of the boys held the horse with its head facing to Birkenhead, that is, the direction from which it had just come, as he was told to do, but a customer came out later and reprimanded him in no uncertain terms for having the horse facing into the wind. Despite protestations from the boy, the man took the bridle and turned the horse to face the other way, whereupon it immediately trotted off homewards to beyond Clatterbridge without any passengers! Needless to say, the boy did not get his ha'penny that night.

Those who did not have their own transport would instruct a 'Cabby' to take them as far as The Travellers' Rest. Sometimes three or four of 'The Lads' who had had a Saturday night out in Birkenhead

The Traveller's Rest with some of the boys from the village

after visiting The Argyle would do this. The Cabby, of course sat on the seat on the back, outside the cab. It was quite a long pull from Birkenhead, up Borough Road, Mount Road, and as it got steeper the horse slowed and the Cabby nodded off. When they were sure the Cabby was asleep, one by one they 'dropped off' the cab as it got near to the village, and then when the horse stopped through habit at The Travellers' Rest the Cabby woke with a start to find there was no-one left to pay the fare!

Later in its life, The Travellers' Rest Darts Club was very active up to the 1950's. In 1947 they won the Bebington Darts League First Division and the "Snake Cup". Each year they had an outing, generally described as 'the henpecked husbands' day out at the races'. This was preceded by a 'procession' from the end of School Lane up to the Inn, with "MacNamara's Band" leading. The band was made up of Club members; Jacky Jones led it with a goat mascot, loaned from Bates Farm at Storeton. The leader of the band was Frank Jones playing the accordian, and George Williams on the big drum; he only needed one stick for this,- it only had one side. Traditionally, the parade was 'inspected' by Charlie Griffiths from the Dairy as it passed. Transport would be provided by one of Mr Ollerhead's coaches. Early in the 1900's Mr Charles Ollerhead started the first 'bus' service between New Ferry and Moreton Shore, fare 2d. This was an open 12 seater 'Vulcan' charabanc with solid tyres. After WW1 he got some Thornycroft vehicles to use.

The Travellers' Rest was the pickup point in the village and this provided the first connection between Higher Bebington and Birkenhead. Prior to this it meant a walk to Prenton Road West to catch the tram. This service was mainly on Saturdays. Mr Ollerhead had several buses, and he also ran day trips,-for instance to Blackpool with Mr Sidney Ollerhead driving. There was little chance of outings in those days, so these and the chance to go to Neston Ladies' Day Parade were really grand events. On the longer trips, Mr 'Paddy' Rice playing his accordian is well remembered. With these buses it also meant that the Sunday School could have annual outings as far as New Brighton. Other outings for the children were to Barnston Dale. They would go in the morning, take a few jam butties and a bottle of water, to spend the day there. There was a slide down the side of the hill that they

'Macnamara's Band' on parade in Village road. Note the 'Tin Chapel' in the background

could go down on mats. Those who had already spent all their pennies on rides or other things would wait at the bottom to take the mats back to the top of the hill and be given a free ride for doing it.

8

To the Southern end of the Parish

As we go along Mount Road from the Travellers' rest, we pass five houses and then come to the reclaimed area where the Higher Bebington quarries were, before reaching an S-Bend in the road. From this point, on our left, marking the boundary between the Higher Bebington quarries and the delph belonging to the Stanleys is the path that went to Prospect Hill, now Derwent Road. Under the middle of this bend was the tunnel through which the Storeton Tramway ran taking stone to the quay on the inlet from the Mersey. During WW2 use was made of this tunnel as an Air-Raid shelter.

Wishing-Gate

We then come to the junctions of Bracken Lane and Rest Hill Road with Mount Road. This part was considerably widened on the right hand side after the junction when the field on the Southwestern corner was sold and a house built there in the 1930's. Prior to this there was a farm gate on that corner, the conifers were not planted until the house was built, so there was a wonderful view across Wirral and into North Wales from here. Whichever way you approached this point, it was an ideal place to stop, look, take in the view before moving on. It became known as "The Wishing Gate"; the name perpetuated in that of the house. The 'original' gate, rather delapidated, was taken and preserved at the house for very many years.Perhaps it was the enchantment of the view that stirred people's thoughts, to make this "The Wishing Gate". Here you wished for your heart's desire and, as with other wishes, you told no-one or your wish never came true.

Couples stopped here, held hands through the bars of the gate to make their wish, to plight their troth; though so much changed, it is a

'The Wishing Gate'

spot that still stirs memories for many people in Wirral.The Wishing Gate was immortalised by the poet-artist John Foster Pride in his poem "The Wishing Gate at Bebington", which he illustrated with his own engravings of the gate and the view at the head, and Higher Bebington Mill at the foot, and he printed it on a heavy cream paper in a limited edition. On the Eastern side of the road, opposite Wishing Gate, is Brackenwood Park. Let's go and have a look there.

Brackenwood

Now a Public Park that is almost entirely devoted to a Golf course, this was the site of a lovely house built of local stone, and its gardens. Most of the gardens remain in substantially their original form though the house has long gone. Although there were Tea-rooms at the house for a while after it was bought by the Council, no specific use could be found for the house as a whole, so it was demolished in 1959. The out-buildings remain and now house maintainance facilities for the park.

In 1882 Mr John James Evans bought land that was to accommo-date the house, gardens and several acres of meadow land stretching to

Brackenwood House in the early 1900's

the South. Mr Evans was a Grandson of John Evans of Welshpool who had founded the pharmaceutical company that was to become Evans Medical Ltd, who have factory and offices at Speke. He had introduced the company's products to Canada some twenty years earlier and in 1902 he became Chairman of the Liverpool based operations under the name of Evans Sons, Lecher and Webb Ltd.

John James Evans brother-in-law, who himself was also a grandson of the founder John Evans, was Sir Aston Webb C.B., C.V.O., P.R.A., the architect who had designed the company's building in Bartholomew Close, London in 1879. It was natural then that he should be asked to design a house appropriate to the site, and to his brother-in-law's family requirements.Those who remember the house will know what a creditable job Sir Aston made of the task. The house, sited just to the North of the remaining sunken garden, commanded magnificent views across Wirral, into Lancashire and into the Clwyd range of North Wales. Sir Aston's designs were reproduced and appraised in "The Building News" for 8th July 1884. The stone to build the house was quarried on the site; the remains of the partly filled quarry can still be seen serving as a small car-park at the extreme Northwestern corner of the estate at the top of Bracken Lane. By 1889 the house was completed. To run the house, Mr Evans had a Butler, a Housekeeper/Cook and a Maid, also a Coachman and two Gardeners.

The Evans family remained at Brackenwood until the early 1920's but were remembered in the village for many years after they left, as they involved themselves very much in its life, particularly with welfare work through the Church. It is remembered both by older residents and some of those who were 'in service' at the house that the village children called at the kitchen door after school to collect surplus milk that might be available. When a new baby was born to a village family the father, or one of the older children, could take a basin to the cook and she would provide a meal for them to take home; this was often generous enough to last two days.

Miss Evans held Bible Classes at the house and was a Parish Visitor for the Church. Each visitor covered a district within the Parish and helped those with families in their area. At Christmas time all the cottages in their area were visited; for each family Miss Evans took a piece of pork and some vegetables, a plum pudding, and a new red petticoat for the lady of the house.

It is appropriate at this point to deviate from the story of Brackenwood itself, and mention another aspect of social work in this pre-Welfare State era. Let us look at the conditions and needs as they were then. Following hard on the Industrial Revolution, workers and their families realised the need for provision of security in times of unemployment and sickness, and even to provision for the inevitable, and often early, funeral expenses, to say nothing of the care of the family following the loss of the breadwinner. Insurances as we know them today were unknown for the vast majority of the population, and Unemployment and Sickness Benefits from the State unimagined. The answer as far as most working people were concerned lay in the "Friendly Societies".There were many of these organisations, often limited to particular areas or types of industry, which were established, often by the communities involved themselves and being named to indicate the Trades or Industries for whose workers they provided benefits in these times of need, in return for regular subscriptions. Others took what might appear to be somewhat 'romantic ' names, but these were frequently based on Scriptural allusions to the help they were set up to give. To give further indications of 'local' involvement, their operations were generally based on the operation of 'Lodges' to provide the intimate contacts that would instil yet further a feeling of involvement and security. These Lodges often operated on a Pseudo-secret society basis, with many social activities and fund raising events. Weekly subscriptions would be collected at a Club-room on a set evening of the week. and a specific knock on the door or password frequently had to be given to obtain admission. On special occasions, such as Whit Monday, there would be great events based on a local 'Walk'.

In Higher Bebington the Society was "The Loyal Order Of Ancient Shepherds (Ashton Unity) Friendly Society".There were Lodges throughout the United Kingdom. Their Lodge was established at the National Schools, in School Lane, on 15th October 1864. It must have played a full role Nationally, for in 1886 Mr Ledsom of Bebington was the National Chief Shepherd. This Lodge remained, but in later years was at Victoria Hall until 1954 when, because of diminishing numbers from the changing social conditions, it was transfered to Harwarden as

The Loyal Order of Ancient Shepherds on their walk with the band

a combined North Wales and West Cheshire District Lodge, with a total membership of only 38. Whilst the Lodge was in the village, Whit-Monday was their 'Big Day'. Members assembled either at the old schools or Victoria Hall and preceded by the Band, this was generally either the Bromborough or, in later years, the Port Sunlight band and the Club Banners the 'walk' started. This covered the village part of the Parish to include calls at 'the Big Houses', principal of these would be Brackenwood. Here refreshments would be taken, contributions

The Loyal Order of Shepherds in the gardens of Brackenwood House

A 'Crook-head from the Staffs that were carried by Officers of the Society

received from the house and in their later years a photograph taken of the whole asembly in the grounds. This gave a splendid record of the day; the Band, Banners, various Officers of the Society carrying their Staffs in the form of a brass topped 6 foot Shepherd's crook, with members wearing their Lodge sashes. The Vicar and his wife always accompanied the walk and they, with members of the Evans family, would be prominent on the front row. The walk continued down Bracken Lane, calling at Gorsey Hey and back to Victoria Hall for dinner at midday. In passing King's farm to go to Victoria Hall, as noted when we talked of the farm, the Pig would be put on the wall 'To Watch The Band Go By'. In the afternoon there would be sports and all the fun of the Fair on Tyson's Field, and in the evening, dancing in Victoria Hall to round things off.

The Evans left Brackenwood in the early 1920's when the house passed to Sir George Carter, the Managing Director of Camell Lairds, the ship builders. Unfortunately, Sir George died only a few years later and

"Putting the Pig in the Wall to watch the Band Go By" at Smailes' Farm

the house was leased by Captain Jacobs of the Jacobs Biscuit Company in Liverpool until 1930, when the house and its land were purchased by Bromborough and Bebington Urban District Council, to be transformed into the public park, more or less as we know it today. The initial purchase was of 8 acres in 1929 and a further 24 acres soon afterwards. The park was formally opened on the evening of 28th May 1931 by Mr J.J.R.Brown, Chairman of the Parks Committee. The field area to the South was set out as a Public Golf Course, in replacement of the one on the land on the Northern side of the top of Town Lane, along King's Road as far as the Church which was developed for housing in 1930/31. In 1971 the golf course area was further extended when the Council purchased the Needwood Farm property and developed it as part of the Brackenwood Park.

If we walk down the path that slopes away from the house to the East, we come to a Lodge House on Bracken Lane. For about 13 years before Brackenwood became a park, Mr Herbert Tavener and his family lived here. Mr Tavener's father, Mr W.H.Tavener, had a wholesale grocery business in Liverpool; this son, Herbert, in partnership with a Mr Rutledge who provided the capital for the venture, bought the confectionary side of the business and so founded the company of Tavener Routledge, sweet manufacturers.

Needwood Farm.

As we leave Brackenwood through the park and cross Brackenwood Road we are on the extension of the Golf Course which was set out in 1971 where Needwood Farm stood. This was the last working farm in the Parish, and formed its Southernmost extremity. The main farmhouse, well designed and brick-built with extensive cellars to which much thought had obviously been given, gave the impression of being a Gentleman's residence of quality. This house was probably a later addition to the properties, the original farm house was likely to have been the cottage adjacent to it which had been enlarged by taking in the tack-room and other parts that would have been earlier working areas. Certainly the working buildings were extensive and comprehensive, suggesting that it had been refurbished during the previous hundred years.

Needwood Farm, shortly before it was closed and incorporated into Brackenwood Park.

On maps drawn up in the 19th century the 'Needless Inn' is also marked as being on the same site. Details of this are hard to find, and it seems to have disappeared well before living memory of even the oldest inhabitants. It is difficult to imagine who it would serve, it was away from the road so would not get passing traffic, and even locally it was rather remote. The farm is remembered from when it was tenanted by Mr Thomas Davis, 'Fat Tom' as he was better known. He was a very portly figure, believed to weigh well over 20 stone. To travel around he had a specially adapted landau, the folding steps of which were adapted to serve as a seat so that he could sit down while talking to his workers in the fields. He is also remembered for introducing steam-ploughing to the area. This involved having, at each side of the field, a large traction engine that had a winding-drum underneath it on which there was a heavy cable that would haul a reverible, multiple plough backwards and forewards across the field. This greatly speeded up the ploughing.

Going up Brackenwood Road, this part of which used to be called

Gipsy Lane, towards the Brackenwood Estate we come to the corner with Peter Price's Lane, here there was another small farm tenanted by Jim Corfe. It has long gone, but up till about 1980 traces of its foundations could be seen. Opposite the farm lived Alf Jones who was Huntsman with the Royal Rock Beagles; he had the kennels there and looked after the pack.

Gorsey Hey.

As we come back through Brackenwood Estate, we join the Heath Road-Tee Hey Lane junction where Gorsey Hey stood. It is now the Elim Christian Rest Home. In 1862 Andrew Tucker Squarey, who in 1868 became the first Solicitor to the newly formed Mersey Docks and Harbour Board, a position he held until shortly before he died in 1900,bought this triangle of land of just over 2 acres, together with a further 7 acres on the South side of Heath Road. On the 2 acre plot he had a house built of the local stone, for his family, and they moved in from their house in Lower Bebington the following year.

Mr Squarey had eleven surviving children from his two marriages, and they were educated by visiting tutors from Liverpool. The billiard

Gorsey Hey with the later addition of a third floor

room in the basement was used as a school-room. Their Father insisted that they each learned to play a musical instrument, or to sing, and Sunday evenings were spent in the large lounge (there were two) having musical entertainment.

Mr Squarey knew Mr Mayer of Lower Bebington, and loaned pictures and other works of art from his collection for exhibitions which Mr Mayer arranged. The house was sold when Mr Squarey died, to Mr Tillotson and then later to Mr George Eaton. Both these gentlemen were closely involved with the Boy's Club at the school. It was sold in 1917 to Mr William Gibbons Henderson, "Silk Mercer" of Church Street, Liverpool, that is of "Henderson's" shop. He sold it in 1922 to Mr Frank Arthur Reece, "Milk Contractor", of Liverpool, or as is remembered, "Reeces" restaurants. The 7 acres along Heath Road was sold in two parts to Bebington Council and Bolton's the builders for housing development.

In 1925 the house was converted and became a Hotel until 1950, and it was probably during this time that the additional top storey which most people remember it having, was added. This, unfortunately, whilst increasing its accommodation did not fit in well with its general architecture.Then, until the early 1990's it was a Masonic Hostel, before it was sold for redevelopement to its present use.

Fir-Bob Land

9

Higher Bebington Hall

We return along Tee Hey Lane, through the centre of the village, until we see King's Close on our left, just before Broadway. King's Close and Mount Park, together with Mount Avenue and Mount Way form quite a considerable estate that occupies much of the site of the former Higher Bebington Hall and its park-lands. However, until 1963 when Higher Bebington Hall was to be sold by Birkenhead Corporation, many people were unaware of its existance, as it stood back from the road in a well wooded area, and the drive entrance was a quite unpretentious feature. At the time the Hall was built, the drive to it was from Dacre Hill and was the full length of what is now King's Lane. The entrance on King's Road was only put in place when King's Lane was developed for housing, and King's Road 'Made-up and Adopted'.

The Hall had been built by George King in 1840. Until then he and his family had lived at "Heath Cottage" in Birkenhead, at that time in a quiet country setting, but what is now very close to the Western part of the Birkenhead Docks. That area was then rapidly developing and it is on record that George King "was offered a fancy price for the property". His Father, Bryan, had been the Rector of Woodchurch and his Mother the Patron of that Living. His Mother's Antecedents from the middle of the 16th C included 6 Rectors, 2 Curates- in-Charge and 9 Patrons of Woodchurch. Various lands and properties in the Oxton and Woodchurch areas were owned by members of the King family. George King's wife, Catherine Ashfield, was descended on her Father's side from Richard Ashfield of Butten's Hall in Hornchurch, Essex, who had been a Colonel in the Parliamentary Army and received the Freedom of Ayr in 1656. Her Mother's family were

Higher Bebington Hall, built by George King about 1840.

Christ's Church, prior to the building of the tower and spire in 1884.

descended from the Morris's, originally from Tinton, Monmouth who had held offices such as Colonial Governor of New Jersey and Judge of Admiralty in New York Province. However, such was their British patriotism that following the American Declaration of Independence, they returned to this country in the early 1780's.

George and Catherine were married in 1809; they had five children. Of these, Vincent Ashfield had an Army career, becoming a Colonel. He gave generously when his Father proposed the Church be built, and the tower and spire were given in his memory by his widow and family in 1886. George Smith King married Lucy Marwood Willis whose Father was the joint promoter with George King for the building of Christ Church. Ellen married Harvey Goodwin who had a distinguished career in the Church, becoming Bishop of Carlisle; their daugther Frances Wycliff married William Archibald Spooner, who was Dean of New College Oxford, and later became an honorary Canon of Christ Church, Oxford. He is widely remembered for his lapses of speech which became known as 'Spoonerisms'. The house was built of local stone, with an East facing Palladian frontage the columns of which were each single pieces of stone, subtilely tapered. This looked over extensive lawns to a modest lake. There were all the ancilliary buildings one would expect for a house of that calibre of those days. There was a large walled yard at the rear of the house and just outside this were capacious, solidly built stone pig-styes, to ensure the supply of meat and bacon. When the house was partly demolished, it was evident that in the large kitchen was a substantial, built-in slate-topped table on stone pillars. From the general form of this and the channels on the floor leading to a central drain, a local butcher gave the opinion that this was specifically for the dressing of pig carcasses.

There was a coach house and stabling; even these were built of large individual blocks of local stone, rather than smaller pieces. The stables were well fitted out for at least four horses, with elegantly designed wrought iron work fittings. The ladder in the stables was of interest, it was not made in the usual form, but was a single, sustantial board with strengthening rails fixed on the back along each side and, rather that rungs, there were alternating foot-holes at about 9" intervals. Very soon after moving to the Hall, Ellen King started a 'Saturday

School' for the children of the village. This was to take the place of a Sunday School, as the King family always went over to Woodchurch on Sundays and it was a long walk for the children to the then Parish Church, St Andrew's and even further to the new church, St Peter's in Rock Ferry. This was held in the room over the coach-house at the Hall which had been fitted out for this by Ellen's brother George and their Mother.

George King remained at the Hall until his second wife died, and then his brother-in-law, William Valient Willis, who had till then lived in Rock Park, went to live there. He was a merchant and insurance broker in the firm of Woolfall, Willis & Co. Later, Mr Hodgson lived at the Hall. He was appointed to the Managing Body of the Schools under the 1902 Education Act, by the Urban District Council. Soon after WW1 it was bought by Birkenhead Corporation. It was then leased to members of the Clarke family who were the Proprietors of the Argyle Theatre in Birkenhead. They lived there from 1921 until 1963. During that time many of the Stars of the 'Old' Music Hall were entertained there when they came to appear at the Theatre.

Christ's Church.

Higher Bebington was part of the large Parish of Bebington. The growth of the Rock Ferry area in the early part of the 19th C led to the setting up of a Chapel there to cater for the new members of the Parish. In 1844 the new Church of St Peter's in Rock Ferry was built as a more permanent Daughter Church to St Andrew's, but this was further away from the old village of Higher Bebington than was St Andrew's.

In the 1850's Mr George King, his brother the Revd Joshua King, Rector of Woodchurch, and Mr William Valient Willis, George King's brother-in-law gave the land on which a new church was to be built in the village, on what is now King's Road. They also gave the stone from the local quarries for its construction and other members of their families and land-owners subscribed to the cost. A detailed description of the Church, with an account of its planning, building and history until 1989 is given in "Christ Church Higher Bebington: 1859-1989" by the author, and only an outline is given here.

The Church is in the Early English style, designed by Walter Scott the architect of many properties, including his own house, in Wirral. The foundation stone was laid by Mrs Willis on 1st August 1857 and the finished Church Consecrated by Bishop John Graham of Chester on Christmas Eve 1859.

The entrance porch, tower and the wooden shingled spire are later additions, given by Elizabeth King as a memorial to her husband Vincent Ashfield King who had been a substantial benefactor to the Church. There was originally a bronze cockerel weather-vane which capped the spire but this was not replaced during repairs to the spire in 1957 because of shortage of funds.

The single 'Calling-bell' which originally hung on the outer East wall of the Church was moved into the tower when it was built. The tower also contains a carillion of eight bells played from a keyboard; this is a memorial to those of the village who lost their lives in WW1. In 1899 a fine specimen of the prehistoric footprints from the quarries that had provided the stone for the Church was placed in the wall of the tower, opposite the main door. The overall lines of the interior are clean, lofty and uncluttered. The high roof is supported by curved scissor-beams of laminated timbers. In the nave the corbels are plain, in keeping with the overall simplicity, but are decorated in the aisles. The columns supporting the clerestory walls are of single pieces of local free-stone.

The font, of Caen stone, was the gift of the Revd Philip Robin, Rector of Woodchurch, and his wife, when the Church was built. It was originally near the North door, where the book cupboard is now, but was moved to its present position about 1914 to give a more clearly defined area for the Baptistry. In the North aisle is the memorial Chapel to the Revd Leslie Troughton, the second Vicar of the Parish; it was made by Hems to the design of Charles Deacon in 1925. The pulpit was moved Northwards by about 6 feet to its present position when the Chancel Screen and Rood, also by Hems to Deacon's design, were installed in 1912 as a memorial to Mr & Mrs Harding. The carving is in oak, and the Rood was gilded in 1979 to enhance its impact.

In the Chancel the roof beams are supported on finely carved corbels depicting angels holding Fruits of the Earth or at Prayer. The choir-stalls were given in memory of Mary Ellen Nickels in 1912. The original small Vestry was extended in 1906 as a memorial to the first

Interior of the church before the road was installed

Vicar, the Revd George Troughton, to accommodate the choir which had then become an established part of the Church.

On the North side is a fine organ by Rushworth and Dreaper, dedicated in February 1927; and well maintained by them ever since it continues to show its excellent qualities. The Reredos, a memorial to Christopher Rawden in 1880, carries finely carved panels with the Chi Rho Sigma and Iota Eta Sigma motifs surrounded by vines and wheat. The Altar was given by the Communicants of the Parish to commemorate the 50th anniversary of the Church. It is the work of Griffiths to designs by Hastwell Grayson, showing the Pascal Lamb in the centre panel. The East window by Willford was installed in 1951 to replace the original that was destroyed by enemy action in WW2. The West window is the original by Edmundson, the gift of Matthew Marwood Willis at Christmas 1862. All the windows in the North aisle are by Morris. A full description of the windows is given in the book about the Church.

Although Higher Bebington is no longer a quarrying or farming village it still retains its individuallity. I feel that the combination of its growth and its fellowship is well shown when the Church is decorated for Harvest Festival. It shows us our roots, needs and continuing life in Higher Bebington, indeed , of all similar communities.

Fir-Bob Land

Epilogue

I said at the beginning that I was not a Fir-Bob, but I have talked with many of them over the years. One of them gave me the following Recipe which I think says a lot about Fir-Bobs as I have come to know them.

Fir-BobPie

1 Measure of Fir-Bobs
1 Cup of Joy
1 Cup of Happiness
A Large Measure of Trust
2 Oz Gladness
1 Pint of Faith
1 Large Slice of *Love.*

Carefully blend together the Fir-Bobs with Joy, Happiness, Trust, Gladness and Love. Add a Pint of Faith, mix with the Hand of Friendship. Cook at the temperature of Warm Fellowship, until the top is the colour of Golden Sunshine. Finish off with a liberal sprinkling of Wit and Humour, cut into generous portions with a Ray of Hope. One portion a day, along with the Love of God, will bring Peace and Happiness.